# ORTHO'S All About

# Finish Carpentry
### Basics

Meredith® Books
Des Moines, Iowa

Ortho® Books
An imprint of Meredith® Books

*Ortho's All About Finish Carpentry Basics*
Editor: Larry Johnston
Contributing Writer: John Riha
Art Director: Tom Wegner
Assistant Art Director: Harijs Priekulis
Copy Chief: Catherine Hamrick
Copy and Production Editor: Terri Fredrickson
Book Production Managers: Pam Kvitne,
    Marjorie J. Schenkelberg
Contributing Copy Editor: Steve Hallam
Technical Proofreader: Ray Kast
Contributing Proofreaders: Debra Morris Smith, Lisa Stone,
    JoEllyn Witke
Indexer: Barbara L. Klein
Electronic Production Coordinator: Paula Forest
Editorial and Design Assistants: Kathleen Stevens,
    Karen Schirm

Additional Editorial Contributions from
    Art Rep Services
Director: Chip Nadeau
Designer: lk Design
Illustrator: Dave Brandon

Meredith® Books
Editor in Chief: James D. Blume
Design Director: Matt Strelecki
Managing Editor: Gregory H. Kayko
Executive Ortho Editor: Larry Erickson

Director, Retail Sales and Marketing: Terry Unsworth
Director, Sales, Special Markets: Rita McMullen
Director, Sales, Premiums: Michael A. Peterson
Director, Sales, Retail: Tom Wierzbicki
Director, Sales, Home & Garden Centers: Ray Wolf
Director, Book Marketing: Brad Elmitt
Director, Operations: George A. Susral
Director, Production: Douglas M. Johnston

Vice President, General Manager: Jamie L. Martin

Meredith Publishing Group
President, Publishing Group: Christopher M. Little
Vice President, Finance & Administration: Max Runciman

Meredith Corporation
Chairman and Chief Executive Officer: William T. Kerr
Chairman of the Executive Committee: E.T. Meredith III

Photographers
(Photographers credited may retain copyright ©
to the listed photographs.)
L = Left, R = Right, C = Center, B = Bottom, T = Top
King Au/Studio Au: 22T, 92
Baldwin Photography: front cover, 14B, 18, 22C, 26
Laurie Black: 44–45
George deGennaro: 79
Ed Gohlich: 58
Bob Hawks: 30B
Hetherington Photography: 3T, 16–17, 20B, 24T, 24B, 28B,
    29, 32, 34T, 74B, 82
Wm. Hopkins: 25, 28T, 75, 86, 89
Inside Out Studio: 6, 7T, 7C, 7B, 9, 12, 15, 20T, 30T, 33,
    35B, 36, 42, 52
Jenifer Jordan: 74T, 74C
Peter Krumhardt: 35T
Dean Tanner: 34B
Rick Taylor: 68
James Yochum: 78, 80

All of us at Ortho® Books are dedicated to providing you
with the information and ideas you need to enhance your
home and garden. We welcome your comments and
suggestions about this book. Write to us at:
    Meredith Corporation
    Ortho Books
    1716 Locust St.
    Des Moines, IA 50309–3023

If you would like more information on other Ortho
products, call 800-225-2883 or visit us at www.ortho.com

**Note to the Readers:** Due to differing conditions, tools,
and individual skills, Meredith Corporation assumes no
responsibility for any damages, injuries suffered, or losses
incurred as a result of following the information published
in this book. Before beginning any project, review the
instructions carefully, and if any doubts or questions remain,
consult local experts or authorities. Because codes and
regulations vary greatly, you always should check with
authorities to ensure that your project complies with all
applicable local codes and regulations. Always read and
observe all of the safety precautions provided by
manufacturers of any tools, equipment, or supplies,
and follow all accepted safety procedures.

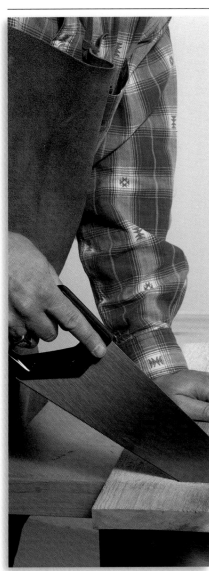

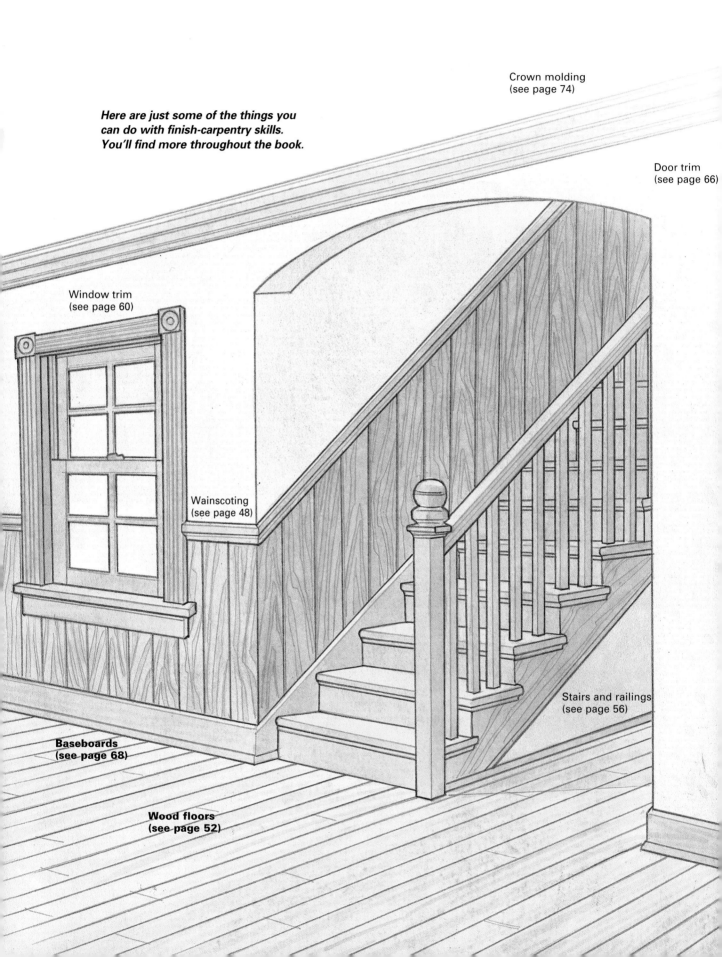

Crown molding
(see page 74)

*Here are just some of the things you
can do with finish-carpentry skills.
You'll find more throughout the book.*

Door trim
(see page 66)

Window trim
(see page 60)

Wainscoting
(see page 48)

Stairs and railings
(see page 56)

Baseboards
(see page 68)

Wood floors
(see page 52)

# MATERIALS FOR FINISH CARPENTRY

*Finish carpentry represents the final stages of a building or remodeling project. The work is precise, with more exacting tolerances and smaller margins for error than in framing and other general carpentry. Careful measurements, a steady hand, an eye for detail, and patience are the hallmarks of a good finish carpenter.*

*A homeowner may elect to do finish work for several reasons. First, it's a good way for a competent homeowner to make a hands-on contribution to a project. For the most part, the materials used are small, lightweight, and easily handled. The do-it-yourselfer saves on labor costs, too. Finally, finish carpentry tasks fit into a homeowner's busy schedule. With the structure enclosed and insulated, and basic systems such as electricity and plumbing operational, a homeowner can take whatever time is needed to hang trim and add decorative details without worrying about the comfort or safety of others in the household.*

*Your first step toward gaining the skills and knowledge necessary to complete top-quality work is to become familiar with the materials. Understanding the characteristics of various materials ensures a smooth and safe job, wastes less time and material, and results in better looking joinery.*

Douglas fir

Redwood

Basswood

# WOOD BASICS

Finish carpentry can be classified as either paint-grade or finish-grade work. Paint-grade work is usually done with a softwood, such as pine; finish-grade work usually calls for a hardwood, such as oak, which will be stained or clear-finished.

**PAINT-GRADE WOODS:** Softwoods, usually used for paint-grade work, cut readily, nail easily, and usually are cheaper than finish-grade wood of the same dimension. Paint adheres well to softwoods, too. Paint-grade also refers to installation techniques and tolerances. Because the wood will be painted, small blemishes, cracks, hammer marks, and slightly misaligned joints can be concealed with fillers before the paint goes on. Novice finish carpenters should hone their skills with paint-grade projects before attempting to work with woods that are to be stained or clear-finished.

**FINISH-GRADE WOODS:** Hardwoods with distinctive grain patterns are the best choice here. These woods often are more difficult to cut, nail, and install. Finish-grade work calls for careful measuring, marking, and cutting because imperfections are difficult to conceal. Dense woods such as oak require predrilling for nails to prevent splitting the wood, making the work time-consuming. Finish-grade woods usually cost more than paint-grade woods.

Hard- or medium-density wood is sometimes used for paint-grade work. A good example is a chair rail, which must withstand occasional bumps and bangs.

Douglas fir, plentiful in western states, is used both as a paint-grade and a finish-grade wood. How a medium-density wood gets used often depends on its availability, its price compared to other woods, and its appearance. Many medium-density woods offer a compromise of workability, price, and natural beauty. These woods also provide good paint-grade surfaces.

## BUYING WOOD

Home improvement centers offer softwoods and hardwoods in many sizes and widths. Lumberyards generally serve the building trades so they are usually well stocked with common pine, fir, and oak. Woodworking specialty stores carry a broad selection of common and exotic hardwoods and provide top-quality boards at premium prices. These stores are usually found only in larger metropolitan areas.

Lumber with both edges and both faces planed smooth at the mill is called S4S (surfaced on four sides). S4S boards usually have slight ripples on the surfaces. These planer marks, left by planing machines at the mill, will show if they aren't sanded out before painting or finishing.

Don't take lumber dimensions literally. For example, a 1×6 board actually measures ¾×5½ inches. The size of an individual board may vary from that standard by ¹⁄₁₆ inch or more. At woodworking specialty stores, you may find unsurfaced boards as well as some that have planed faces and rough edges, called S2S (surfaced on two sides). Although the price may be right, rough lumber and S2S boards require planing and sawing to make them ready for use.

Always measure carefully when estimating wood for a project. When shopping for wood, examine individual boards carefully and reject those with defects such as splits, warpage, cupping, or loose knots.

## SOFT-TEXTURED WOODS

**BASSWOOD:** This soft-grained hardwood cuts, shapes, and sands easily. It resists splintering and is a favorite of wood carvers. It has a faint grain pattern and accepts paint readily. Medium cost.

**CEDAR:** Lightweight and strong, cedar is a softwood that comes in many colors, from deep reds to light cream. It is naturally water-resistant and is a favorite for outdoor furniture and fences. It's somewhat expensive to use as a paint-grade finish wood. Medium-high cost.

**PINE:** This softwood is one of the most common woods, available in many regional varieties such as ponderosa, yellow, and sugar. It is durable, yet easy to cut and shape. It makes an excellent paint-grade wood. Low to medium cost, depending on grade.

## SOFTWOODS AND HARDWOODS

In the lumber industry, the terms softwood and hardwood don't actually refer to how soft or hard a wood is. Instead, they make a botanical distinction: Hardwoods, such as oak, maple, or mahogany, come from deciduous trees. Softwoods, such as pine, fir, and cedar, come from trees generally regarded as conifers or evergreens. Some woods classified as softwoods, such as Douglas fir, are dense and hard while some hardwoods, such as basswood, are soft-textured. Balsa, in fact, is a hardwood.

Cherry

Mahogany

Poplar

Cedar

## MEDIUM-DENSITY WOODS

**POPLAR:** This hardwood is plentiful in some regions. Poplar accepts paint well and does not have a distinctive grain, so it makes an excellent paint-grade finish wood. It sometimes has a greenish color. Its density and durability make it a good choice for trim in high-traffic areas such as doorways. Medium cost.

**CHERRY:** Finely figured cherry combines good workability with rich color and appearance to make a premier finish-grade hardwood. It is highly prized by woodworkers and is most likely to be found in a woodworking specialty store. It is generally in good supply and is not considered a rare

Walnut

White oak
(quartersawn)

Cherry

## HIGH-DENSITY WOODS

**MAPLE:** This hardwood is difficult to cut and work. Its toughness makes it a popular choice for flooring. It has a mild grain pattern and creamy yellow color that finishes to a soft, attractive luster. It is prized as a decorative wood for shelving, cabinets, mantels, and other display pieces. High cost.

**WHITE OAK:** A cousin to the more common red oak, this hardwood was widely used for moldings and furniture in the early 1900s. It has come to characterize the styles known as Arts and Crafts, Prairie School, and Mission. At the sawmill, white oak is often quarter-sawn to produce a distinctive grain pattern. It has a yellowish-brown color. Old-house projects often require white oak to match existing woodwork. High cost.

wood. Clear, natural finishes show off the grain and color to best advantage. High cost.

**DOUGLAS FIR:** This tough, versatile softwood features a tight, striped grain of dark red and cream. It grows abundantly in the western U.S. and is widely available. Fir lumber is used for everything from house framing to fine, raised-panel kitchen cabinets. It is easy to work but is brittle; wear gloves when handling it to avoid the small, sharp splinters. Medium cost.

**MAHOGANY:** This popular hardwood varies widely in quality. You'll find inexpensive, light-colored varieties at home improvement centers. Extraordinarily dense and beautifully grained stock is more often available at woodworking specialty stores. Mahogany is easily cut and shaped and can be either painted or clear-finished. Medium to high cost, depending on grade.

Pine

Oak

White oak
(quartersawn)

# TRIM AND MOLDING

Trim and molding—also called millwork—are basic components of finish carpentry. They are among the last elements to be installed during house construction and remodeling. They strongly influence the look and style of rooms and the appearance of decorative projects, such as built-in shelving and mantels.

The two words—trim and molding—are often used interchangeably, even by professionals. The distinction is actually small. Trim describes sets, such as side casings

## EASY STORAGE FOR MOLDINGS

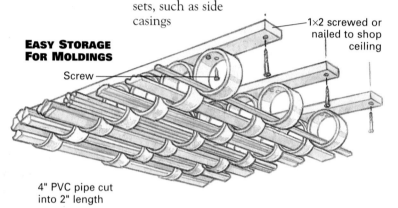

Screw

1×2 screwed or nailed to shop ceiling

4" PVC pipe cut into 2" length

and head casings used to finish doors, windows, closet openings, and built-in units. Moldings are installed horizontally on walls. For this reason, they are sometimes called running moldings. Baseboards and crown are examples of moldings. Mixing up the terms when ordering materials from a supplier probably won't cause confusion.

Millwork is available in paint- and finish-grade. Softwoods such as pine are usually painted, while more decorative hardwoods such as oak are stained or given a clear finish to enhance the appearance of the grain (see Wood Basics, pages 6–7, for more information

about paint- and finish-grade woods). Other species commonly used are poplar, beech, fir, and inexpensive grades of mahogany.

Millwork made of polymers or polyurethane foam is becoming more popular. It is extremely lightweight, easy to handle, and won't crack or splinter. It's as easy to work as pine, and it comes preprimed and ready for paint. It is installed with either nails or glue (see pages 58–77 for more installation information). It doesn't rot, so it is a good choice for exterior applications. Expect to pay about the same for polymer moldings as for good-quality pine.

One common type of molding is finger-jointed millwork. This type is made of many smaller pieces of solid wood that are glued together end to end with strong interlocking joints. The technique was developed as a way for wood mills to make use of smaller pieces of wood that might otherwise be discarded as waste, so it's less expensive than solid wood trim. It should be painted.

Both polymer and finger-jointed millwork can be purchased with a vinyl wrap embossed with a simulated-wood finish. Vinyl-wrapped molding is inexpensive and doesn't need finishing. However, it can't be sanded or shaved to create perfectly fitted joints.

Circle-top windows and curved walls require molding that bends. Wood molding can be bent by sawing a series of vertical kerfs spaced about ½ inch apart along the back of the molding. An easier solution is to purchase flexible polyester molding. If your home improvement supplier or lumberyard doesn't carry it, they can probably special order it for you. It comes in both paint- and stain-grade and can be cut and nailed like wood.

Home improvement centers and lumberyards carry many types and styles of molding and trim at a good price. You can purchase millwork made from hard-to-find wood species, such as walnut or birch, at woodworking specialty stores. You also can use several pieces of stock moldings to create built-up moldings of your own design (see Working with Trims and Moldings, pages 58–77, for more information). A more expensive alternative is to have a custom millwork or cabinet shop make trim or molding to your specifications.

The size of millwork should be in proportion to the size and ceiling height of the room where it is installed. The higher the ceiling, the wider the millwork.

## MATCHING RARE TRIMS AND MOLDINGS

If you want to match elaborate, existing moldings in a historic house, contact a custom millwork or cabinet shop to do the work. First, salvage a piece of the molding. The sample can be short, but the profile—the end view—must be intact. The millwork shop will set up one of its big stationary tools—a shaper—to cut and duplicate your molding. If the shop does not already have the proper shaper knives for matching your profile, custom-made knives can be made to do the job for an additional fee.

**REMOVING ADHESIVE PRICE TAGS FROM LUMBER AND MOLDINGS**

Play heat over tag and board until the tag's adhesive softens, then peel off price tag

Hair dryer set on medium heat

Crown molding

Base molding

Colonial casing

Ranch casing

Base shoe

Corner molding

## MOLDINGS

**BASE:** Installed along the floor, it covers the gap between the wall and the flooring. Base is 3 to 12 inches wide and is either single-piece or built-up—composed of a number of different types of moldings.

**CHAIR RAIL:** Installed 32 to 40 inches off the floor, it protects walls from being dented by chairs and other movable furnishings. But it's more often used as a decorative embellishment that separates two different wall colors or textures, or as part of a wainscoting installation.

**PICTURE RAIL:** This has also become a mostly decorative embellishment. Before the days of easily installed drywall anchors, picture rail was used to hold hooks with wires attached for suspending artwork on walls.

**CROWN MOLDING:** This large molding covers the intersections of walls and ceilings. It is a prominent molding and often plays a major role in giving architectural character to a room.

**CASINGS:** Used to cover the gaps between door or window frames and the surrounding wall surface, today's casings usually have simple profiles. In older houses, they could be elaborate moldings composed of several individual pieces of trim.

**BASE SHOE:** Floors often have dips and bumps that baseboard cannot fully conform to. Base shoe covers the gap between the bottom of the base molding and the floor surface. The smaller, more flexible base shoe adds a finishing touch.

# CREATING STYLE WITH MILLWORK

**STANDARD BUILDER'S MILLWORK**

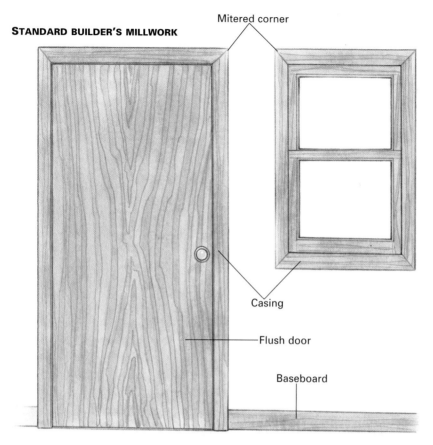

Mitered corner

Casing

Flush door

Baseboard

**ARTS AND CRAFTS MILLWORK**

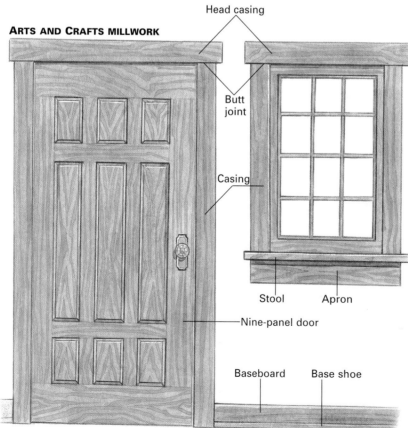

Head casing

Butt joint

Casing

Stool

Apron

Nine-panel door

Baseboard

Base shoe

Trim and moldings greatly affect the character of a room. Size, placement, and the amount of detail in each piece of molding provide visual clues to a home's architectural heritage. The scale of the millwork in relation to the size of the room is one of the most important factors to consider when choosing moldings. Elaborate, complex moldings make a house feel grand and work well in large rooms; simple moldings present soothing, unpretentious interiors and are appropriate for smaller spaces. Studying the looks of moldings in books, magazines, and catalogs is the first step to determining which moldings will work best for your home improvement projects.

**STANDARD BUILDER'S MILLWORK:** This style has simple profiles and is inexpensive. It often goes by the name of ranch or Colonial and is associated with tract homes and suburban houses built during the 1960s and 1970s. It is easy to work with and is easily found in home improvement stores. Its plain style works well as the foundation for vinyl-wrapped moldings and trim.

**ARTS AND CRAFTS MILLWORK:** Plain, square-edged molding made of stain-grade oak—most commonly white, quarter-sawn oak—is associated with Arts and Crafts, Prairie-style, and American foursquare houses from the early 1900s. It is a no-frills ornament without detail or embellishment that works in a variety of settings, including modern suburban homes. Base molding and door and window casings have butt joints and square edges. Crown molding is not a typical feature of the style, but it was a common practice to run a horizontal band of wood molding around the interior of a room 1 to 2 feet below the ceiling to separate wall colors or to hide an indirect lighting scheme.

**TRADITIONAL MILLWORK:**
This style is rooted in classical and romantic homes such as Greek Revival, Colonial, and Italianate houses from the 18th and 19th centuries, and updated versions built during the 1920s and 1930s. The moldings are characterized by elaborate detail, often achieved by building up a single profile from many individual pieces. It takes great skill to plan and install highly decorative traditional moldings. However, they are usually painted, so small gaps and other imperfections can be filled with putty and effectively hidden. Traditional styles look good in many different kinds of today's homes. However, unless you are duplicating a historic scheme, a good rule is to make moldings less elaborate—not more—so the molding won't overwhelm the room.

**VICTORIAN MILLWORK:**
During the late 18th and early 19th centuries, mechanized milling machines made mass production of trims and moldings possible. Many styles of millwork developed during that time are still in use today. Victorian millwork can be paint-grade, but finish-grade is in the original Victorian spirit. The style features many unique types of gingerbread molding, such as spandrels and brackets, that are not found on other house styles. Fortunately, Victorian millwork usually takes advantage of shortcuts, such as corner blocks and plinths, as shown in the illustration at right, that simplify installation. Most modern Victorian-style homes are modified from the older forebears and use less trim. However, the basic tenet for Victorian millwork is "the more the merrier." If you are interested in Victorian millwork, get a catalog from a manufacturer that specializes in the Victorian style.

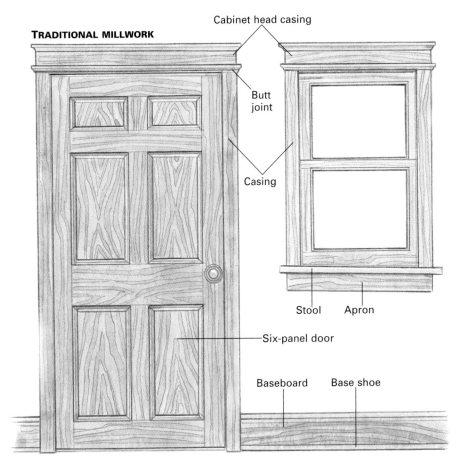

**TRADITIONAL MILLWORK**

Cabinet head casing

Butt joint

Casing

Stool   Apron

Six-panel door

Baseboard   Base shoe

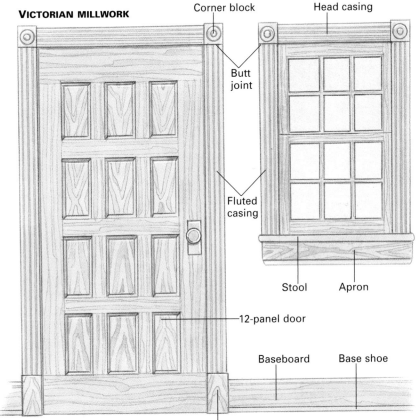

**VICTORIAN MILLWORK**

Corner block   Head casing

Butt joint

Fluted casing

Stool   Apron

12-panel door

Baseboard   Base shoe

Plinth block

# SHEET GOODS AND FASTENERS

Oriented strand board

Plywood (softwood)

Medium-density fiberboard

Melamine-coated MDF

Particleboard

Plywood (hardwood)

Sheet goods, such as plywood, are useful for decorative or structural work. They are easy to cut, and pieces can be joined or installed with glue, nails, or screws. Panels come in thicknesses from ¼ inch to ¾ inch, normally 4 feet wide and 8 feet long. Here are two useful types of sheet goods:

**PLYWOOD:** Strong and dimensionally stable, plywood resists warping and does not split when nailed. Softwood plywood accepts paint well. Plywood that is faced with hardwood veneer provides a suitable surface for staining or clear-finishing. Use plywood to make shelves or as the center panel of frame-and-panel wainscoting (see page 51). Strips of plywood make an excellent backing for built-up moldings (see page 75). Plywood with grooves cut into it simulates the look of board wainscoting or wall paneling and comes prefinished in a variety of colors and wood species. Exposed edges must be covered to hide the laminated layers.

**MEDIUM-DENSITY FIBERBOARD (MDF):** Heavy, hard, and inexpensive, fiberboard works well for concealed parts of cabinets and as solid backing for built-up architectural details. It is sometimes covered with a thin layer of melamine—a plastic.

It lacks strength and is difficult to sand smooth. It cuts easily, although freshly-cut edges are ragged and cannot be smoothed easily. MDF can be used as an inexpensive substitute for real wood if it is painted and its edges are shaped with a router to create crisp details.

## FASTENERS

The standard fastener for finish carpentry is the finish nail— a thin nail with a small head designed to be set beneath the surface.

Typically, the heads are concealed with putty or wood filler. The most common sizes of finish nails are 4d, 6d, and 8d. To prevent denting the workpiece with the hammer head, leave ¼ to ½ inch of the nail above the surface when you drive it. Then sink the head beneath the surface using a nail set (see page 33). Drive a finish nail at least ¾ inch into a framing member or structural piece. The nail must be long enough to pass through nonstructural material such as wallboard. If nailheads won't show, use headed box or common nails for superior holding power.

Fasten thin plywood paneling to solid backing with panel nails. These small nails have ringed shanks for extra holding power. Because the heads are color-matched to the panels, setting the nailheads is unnecessary.

## COVERING PLYWOOD EDGES

Plywood is a versatile material but its edges are unattractive. Using plywood for shelving takes advantage of plywood's strength and low cost but can leave the laminated edges in plain view. Cover the edges by gluing and nailing strips of 1× material to the plywood. One-inch-wide material (1"×¾") adds strength to the shelves. Another way to cover the edges is to apply self-sticking strips of real wood veneer, available in rolls at hardware stores or home improvement centers. Cover exposed edges even if you plan to paint the shelves. Raw edges will not accept paint evenly.

Veneer-faced particleboard

In some cases, you can use screws for finish carpentry. Visible screw heads should be precisely spaced and arranged to look good. Drill holes matched to the size of the screw with a countersink bit (for flathead screws). Brass-headed wood screws are often used when the screw head will be visible.

To conceal a screw, drill the screw hole with a counterbore. The counterbore cuts a hole that accepts a wooden plug to hide the screw head. Drilling countersunk holes, cutting and fitting plugs, and sanding the surfaces smooth is time-consuming work.

To screw together workpieces where screw heads won't show, drive drywall screws with an electric drill equipped with a screwdriver tip. Predrilling holes for drywall screws is unnecessary. However, you should always predrill holes for any screws near the ends of a board.

## HOLE SIZES, STANDARD WOOD SCREWS

|  | Shank Hole | Pilot Hole | | Head |
|---|---|---|---|---|
|  |  | Hardwood | Softwood | Counterbore |
| 2 | $3/32"$ | $1/16"$ | $1/16"$ | $11/64"$ |
| 3 | $7/64"$ | $1/16"$ | $1/16"$ | $13/64"$ |
| 4 | $7/64"$ | $5/64"$ | $1/16"$ | $15/64"$ |
| 5 | $1/8"$ | $5/64"$ | $1/16"$ | $1/4"$ |
| 6 | $9/64"$ | $3/32"$ | $5/6"$ | $9/32"$ |
| 7 | $5/32"$ | $7/64"$ | $3/32"$ | $5/16"$ |
| 8 | $5/32"$ | $7/64"$ | $3/32"$ | $11/32"$ |
| 9 | $11/64"$ | $1/8"$ | $7/64"$ | $23/64"$ |
| 10 | $3/16"$ | $1/8"$ | $7/64"$ | $25/64"$ |
| 12 | $7/32"$ | $9/64"$ | $1/8"$ | $7/16"$ |
| 14 | $1/4"$ | $5/32"$ | $9/64"$ | $1/2"$ |

## HOLE SIZES, DRYWALL/DECK SCREWS

Drill one hole size through both parts to be joined

|  | Hardwood | Softwood | Head |
|---|---|---|---|
| 4 | $5/64"$ | $1/16"$ | $7/32"$ |
| 6 | $7/64"$ | $3/32"$ | $17/64"$ |
| 8 | $1/8"$ | $7/64"$ | $11/32"$ |
| 10 | $9/64"$ | $1/8"$ | $23/64"$ |
| 12 | $5/32"$ | $9/64"$ | $7/16"$ |
| 14 | $3/16"$ | $5/32"$ | $1/2"$ |

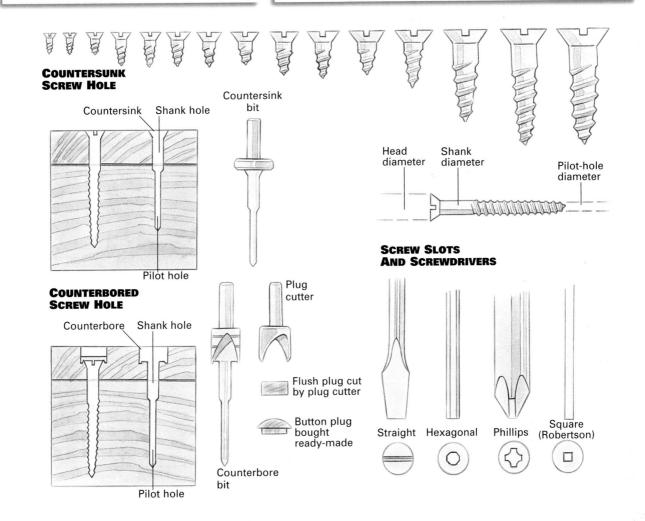

**COUNTERSUNK SCREW HOLE**
Countersink  Shank hole  Countersink bit  Pilot hole

**COUNTERBORED SCREW HOLE**
Counterbore  Shank hole  Pilot hole

Plug cutter
Flush plug cut by plug cutter
Button plug bought ready-made
Counterbore bit

Head diameter  Shank diameter  Pilot-hole diameter

**SCREW SLOTS AND SCREWDRIVERS**
Straight  Hexagonal  Phillips  Square (Robertson)

# ADHESIVES AND ABRASIVES

## GLUE

Glues and adhesives help keep pieces of wood and molding in place and prevent joints from opening up due to wood movement. (All wood moves—changes size slightly—as the amount of moisture in the air changes.) Some projects, such as installing plywood wall paneling, rely on glue almost exclusively. In most cases, however, glue is used in combination with nails or screws. Here are some glues for finish carpentry:

**POLYVINYL ACETATE:** This is the common, inexpensive, nontoxic, water-based white or yellow woodworking glue. Yellow glues hold wood better than white glues. They are suitable only for interior use. Both types tend to soften at temperatures above 110 degrees F, and are not considered to be structural adhesives, such as those used to fasten plywood panels to walls or joists.

**EPOXY:** The two parts of this glue—a resin and a hardener—are mixed together just before use. Epoxies bond almost any material to almost any other, making a strong joint that is almost impossible to separate. Epoxies resist heat, corrosion, shrinkage, and moisture. The glue is widely available but moderately expensive; it's best suited for small jobs requiring a strong, reliable bond.

**CONSTRUCTION ADHESIVE:** This tough, thick glue bonds all types of wood and wood-based building materials together. It usually is applied with a caulking gun, and is often used to install wall paneling. Construction adhesive comes in many grades; most are waterproof. Although other types of glue are easier to apply to moldings, trims, and other small pieces, construction adhesive will bond any of these materials. This adhesive is relatively slow drying; hold the pieces with clamps, nails, or screws until it dries.

**RESORCINOL AND UREA-FORMALDEHYDE:** These strong, waterproof glues are woodworkers' favorites. They come as powders that are mixed with water before use. Because the glue is a dry powder, it can be stored for long periods without adversely affecting its strength. These glues are considered toxic, and must be used in well-ventilated areas.

**CONTACT CEMENT:** Popular for gluing plastic laminates and wood veneers to large surfaces, contact cement bonds instantly and must be used with care. Adhesive is applied to both surfaces to be joined and allowed to dry until tacky. Then the parts are brought together. Precise positioning is essential; once the glued surfaces touch, it is nearly impossible to pull them apart. When practical, cut the laminate or veneer oversize for gluing so that positioning is not as critical. Trim the excess after joining the parts.

**HOT-MELT:** Solid sticks of this plastic glue are heated in an electric glue gun and applied through the gun's tip. Hot-melt glue has a fast adhesion time—typically 30 seconds—but makes a thick glue line and does not create an especially strong bond. Use hot-melt glue for light-duty or temporary bonding.

**CYANOACRYLATE:** Also known as super glue or instant glue, cyanoacrylate adhesive bonds most materials in seconds. It will stick your skin to everything, too; so be careful. It's difficult to use for large glue jobs, but great for small pieces. Thicker varieties—labeled gap-filling—work better on wood.

*Woodworker's yellow glue is versatile and easy to use. Spread glue evenly and clamp the joint for best results. The glue spreader shown is a used foam paintbrush with the foam removed.*

## PRO ADVICE: GLUING WOOD

Always clamp glued joints. When using polyvinyl acetate, construction adhesive, resorcinol, and urea-formaldehyde glues, apply a thin layer of glue evenly to both surfaces to be joined. Then, wait until the glue is tacky before clamping the pieces together. Wipe off excess glue immediately. When the work is dry, sand or scrape the area around the joint to remove any excess glue that may have squeezed out of the joint.

## SANDPAPER

Count on sandpaper to smooth uneven surfaces, remove old finishes, and prepare projects for painting or staining. But don't assume sandpaper will help fix mistakes. It's better to rely on precise measurements and exact cutting than to think of sandpaper as a cure-all for imprecise work. Used improperly, sandpaper will dull details, round off edges, and scratch finish surfaces.

Sand in stages, using progressively finer grits. For rough edges or surfaces, start with a coarse, 80-grit paper. Move to a 120-grit paper to smooth the surface and remove marks left by the 80-grit. This level of sanding is usually adequate for most finish- or paint-grade materials. Use 180- or 220-grit sandpaper on fine hardwoods to achieve a surface that is perfectly smooth to the touch. Cabinetmakers and makers of fine furniture often add yet another step—320-grit.

Always sand with the grain. Even a brief swipe across the grain will leave marks that are difficult to remove. For best results on flat surfaces, use a handheld sanding block. Use power sanders for fast removal of material.

Sandpaper comes in sheets, loops for belt sanders, and disks for palm sanders. There are several kinds of sandpaper available, each with unique properties. However, most will perform adequately for finish carpentry tasks.

**GARNET PAPER:** The reddish-brown cutting surface of this sandpaper is made up of tiny garnet crystals that constantly break during use, creating new, sharp cutting edges. Traditionally, garnet paper is used for hand sanding and fine cabinetmaking.

**FLINT PAPER:** A softer mineral gives this sandpaper its pale, yellowish color. It is the least expensive abrasive paper and tends to wear out quickly. It is best for hand sanding with a sanding block.

**ALUMINUM OXIDE PAPER:** Sheets have a tan color with dark abrasive particles. When made to fit palm sanders or as a loop for belt sanders, aluminum oxide abrasives may have a white or a dark, grayish-purple color. This is a tough, durable paper that is good for general use and works well in electric sanders.

**WET/DRY PAPER:** The dark gray color comes from the silicon carbide abrasives used on the surface. The backing is resistant to moisture, and the paper is sometimes used with a lubricant such as water or mineral spirits to float away grit and help produce a lustrous finish.

Aluminum oxide

Wet/dry

Garnet

*You'll rely on power tools for most of your finish carpentry work, but hand tools, such as this fine-toothed shorty saw, will prove handy sometimes. To saw straight and true with a handsaw, try these tips:*

■ *Extend the index finger of your hand alongside the saw handle. This prevents the saw from turning or twisting in your hand.*

■ *Keep the wrist of the hand holding the saw straight, and move your arm in a straight line from the shoulder in the direction of the cut.*
■ *Watch the reflection of the board in the saw blade. When the reflection appears to run straight through the blade, you're holding the saw straight and making a square cut.*

# TOOLS AND TECHNIQUES

Familiarity with tools and knowledge of how to use them properly are important aspects of finish carpentry. That's because a set of instructions, no matter how thoroughly detailed, cannot completely anticipate your working conditions, the exact materials you'll be using, and your degree of expertise. Being familiar with the tools you own, knowing which tools to use for specific tasks, and understanding how to use them properly are keys to successfully completing a project. With this knowledge, you'll be able to work efficiently, fix any mistakes (a few are inevitable), cope with unusual circumstances, and make adjustments that allow you to produce beautiful results.

As you work, make safety a priority. Using tools—hand or power—requires clear thinking and concentration; don't work when you are tired or distracted. Care for tools by storing them properly, keeping blades sharp, and maintaining power tools according to the manufacturer's directions. If you're not sure how to sharpen cutting edges or service power tools, have a professional do it.

# MEASURING AND MARKING

Accurate measurements are the soul of any finish carpentry project. The old carpenter's adage, "measure twice, cut once," still makes a lot of sense. Take time with measurements, and write down results to ensure you have the correct dimensions when you cut a piece of material to length. The standard for finish carpentry is accuracy of better than $\frac{1}{32}$ of an inch—that's finer than the $\frac{1}{16}$-inch divisions that are the smallest on a standard tape measure. You'll need to be careful—and use a sharp pencil—to measure, mark, and cut boards to such a precise dimension.

If tight-fitting joints are important to you, you'll want to cut your workpiece just slightly too long and test-fit it, then shave the end to create the best-looking work possible. Another way is to back-cut the joints: Cut the joint on a very slight angle—a bevel—so that the rear, unseen portion of the workpiece slopes away from the front. If adjustments are necessary, simply shave or sand very slight amounts from the beveled front of the workpiece to create perfect joinery.

Don't settle for inexpensive measuring tools—get the best products you can afford. They will provide more reliable, precise measurements and will last longer than inexpensive ones. Here are some tools that you will find useful:

**COMBINATION SQUARE:** The head of this versatile square slides on a 1-foot-long rule. The head makes 90-degree (right angle) and 45-degree angles. With the head moved to one end of the rule, the combo square can check inside right angles. Use a combination square to ensure that the blade of a circular saw or table saw is set at 90 degrees. (Unplug the saw before you do this.) The sliding rule is locked in place with a knurled knob in the handle of the tool. It allows the rule to be set in increments for marking jamb reveals and for other marking tasks that require repeating the same measurement.

**TRY SQUARE:** This is similar to the combination square except the rule is fixed, not adjustable. Some carpenters consider the try square to be more reliable for marking and checking square corners and angles.

**SPEED SQUARE:** This lightweight plastic or aluminum triangle quickly establishes square or 45-degree angles. Because of its triangular

## PRO ADVICE: V MARKS THE SPOT

Mark a measurement with a small V, not a single slash. A single, hand-drawn line is never reliably straight, so you might wonder later which end shows the actual measurement. The V, on the other hand, indicates a single point from which to establish a line for cutting or laying out.

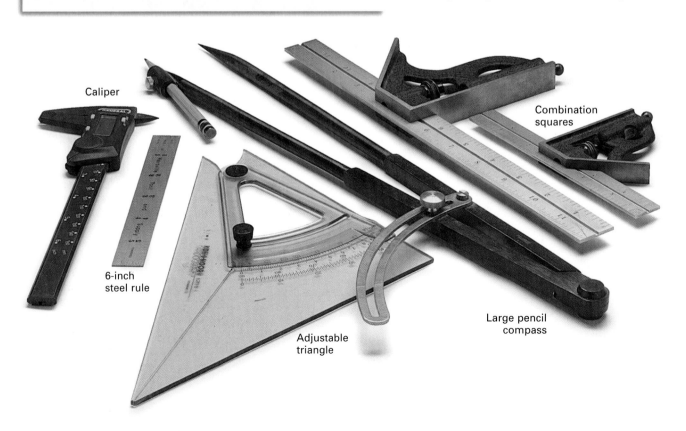

Caliper

6-inch steel rule

Adjustable triangle

Combination squares

Large pencil compass

shape, it is virtually impossible to knock a speed square out of alignment. The speed square features many additional markings that help framing carpenters lay out rafters and stairs, but the tool is also useful for the finish carpenter. Another feature is the thickness of the speed square: The edge makes a handy guide when crosscutting with a circular saw or saber saw.

**DIVIDER:** Sometimes called a compass, this layout tool has two adjustable legs that are held in position by a knurled knob at one side of the tool. The legs have pointed steel tips, or one steel tip and a pencil. Dividers are used for marking circles, but their more important use is for scribing irregular shapes onto moldings or other finish materials so that the materials can be cut for a precise fit. Don't try to use the type of compass usually found in elementary school classrooms—the leg joint is not tight enough to hold the legs in position for accurate scribing.

**CALIPER:** A precision tool used to take precise measurements of smaller objects, such as the thickness of moldings, a caliper has jaws for taking both external and internal measurements and a depth gauge for measuring the depth of cuts and holes. A caliper makes it easy to transfer precise measurements to tools, such as when setting the depth of saw blades or marking on the shank of a drill the depth of holes for dowels. Although a caliper might seem like a specialty tool, it is a handy addition to the finish carpenter's toolbox and provides accurate measurements.

## IS YOUR SQUARE SQUARE?

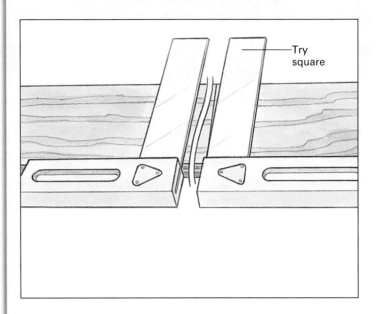

Occasionally, a combination or try square gets out of alignment. If you suspect your square is not marking an absolutely true 90-degree angle, you can check it. You'll need a piece of wood with a straight edge at least twice as long as the handle of your square. Check the edge of the wood for straightness using a level or the blade of a framing square. Set your combination or try square on the wood and draw a line along the blade across the face of the wood. Now turn your square over and draw another line at the same location. If the lines match perfectly, your square is true. If the lines diverge, buy a new one.

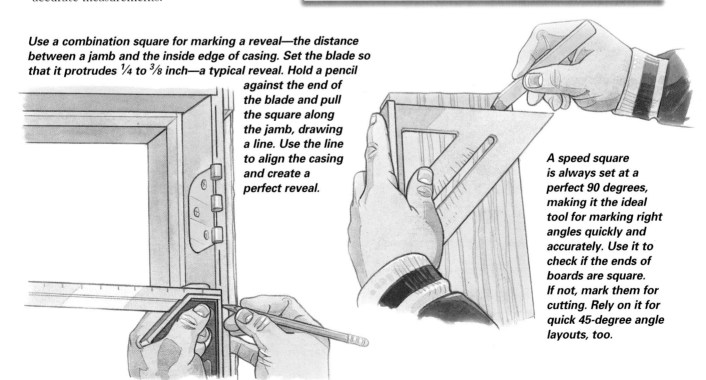

Use a combination square for marking a reveal—the distance between a jamb and the inside edge of casing. Set the blade so that it protrudes ¼ to ⅜ inch—a typical reveal. Hold a pencil against the end of the blade and pull the square along the jamb, drawing a line. Use the line to align the casing and create a perfect reveal.

A speed square is always set at a perfect 90 degrees, making it the ideal tool for marking right angles quickly and accurately. Use it to check if the ends of boards are square. If not, mark them for cutting. Rely on it for quick 45-degree angle layouts, too.

# HANDSAWS

Crosscut saw

Coping saw

Backsaw

*Basic saws for the finish carpenter include a crosscut saw for cutting stock across the grain, a backsaw for making precise, straight cuts in all woods, and a coping saw for cutting curves and intricate designs.*

Handsaws are useful, safe, versatile tools of the finish carpenter. They are lightweight and portable, and they are especially good for making precise, splinter-free cuts in wood moldings and trims. Specialty handsaws can do certain cutting tasks that are virtually impossible to do with a power saw.

Handsaws are classified by the spacing of the teeth—sometimes referred to as points—on the cutting blade. The somewhat confusing rating system refers either to teeth per inch (TPI) or points per inch (PPI). There is always one less tooth per inch than points. For example, a saw rated at 7 TPI equals 8 PPI. When you hear a saw referred to as an 8-point saw, it means 8 PPI.

Handsaws are also specified as crosscut or ripsaws. Crosscut saws cut across the grain of the workpiece; ripsaws cut with the grain. Before power tools became popular, ripsaws were essential. Today, however, almost all rip cuts are done with power saws.

Generally, 6- or 7-point saws are for heavy-duty cutting and rough framing work. Saws with 8 to 10 PPI are for general-purpose cutting. An 11-point or higher saw is used for making fine, precise cuts. For finish work, you should have an 8-point, general-purpose crosscut saw and a 15-point backsaw. A backsaw has a ridge of steel along the back of the blade to stiffen it, making precise cutting easier. A dovetail saw is a small backsaw with very fine teeth. Although its primary use is cutting joints for furniture construction, the dovetail saw makes precise cuts in thin pieces of molding.

Another essential tool for the finish carpenter is a coping saw. It has a stiff, U-shape frame, a thin, fine-toothed, removable blade, and a small handle. It excels at cutting irregular shapes. The depth and complexity of the cut is limited by the distance between the blade and the back of the saw frame. For finish work, use a coping saw to make coped joints—a type of joinery used when two pieces of molding meet at an inside corner. Mastering the coped joint—and using a

## JAPANESE SAWS

Japanese saws are becoming more popular in the U.S. These thin-bladed saws are designed to cut on the pull stroke, not the push stroke like traditional Western saws. Many woodworkers say this prevents the blade from buckling and wobbling, giving the user better control. The thin steel makes the blade flexible, allowing the saw to adapt to specialty tasks. One type, with no tooth set, is the best for cutting off dowels flush with surrounding surfaces. The fine tooth configuration makes the saws difficult to sharpen. As a result, most of these saws have replaceable blades. You can find Japanese saws at most home improvement centers.

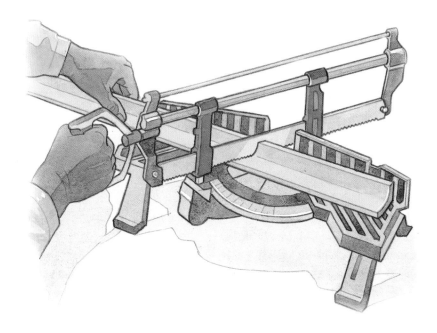

coping saw to do it—is one of the basic skills of finish carpentry.

When making cuts with a handsaw, you need to do two things correctly: One is to follow a marked cutting line and cut the workpiece to the correct length. The other is a bit more difficult—holding the blade of your saw at precisely 90 degrees to the workpiece so that the finished cut is square. One way to do this is to watch the reflection of the workpiece in the blade of your saw (see page 16). If the edge of the actual workpiece and the edge of its reflection form a straight line, you're on target. With practice, you'll make every cut square and true.

Using a hand miter box is one way to ensure that your cuts are square. The miter box can be set to a variety of angles, and the box holds the saw absolutely straight up and down. Although a high-quality hand miter box is an excellent tool, it has been largely replaced by the faster and highly accurate power miter box (see page 22).

*A well-made hand miter box makes precise angled cuts across the grain in molding and trim stock.*

## PRO ADVICE: KEEP IT SHARP

Make sure your saw is sharp; a sharp saw is safer and easier to use and makes better cuts. To check, inspect the tips of the teeth closely. If you see light glinting off the teeth, they're dull. To keep your saw in peak condition, have it sharpened regularly by a professional sharpener. To find a professional nearby, look in the Yellow Pages of your telephone directory under "Saws— Sharpening & Repair." Many hardware stores, lumberyards, and home improvement centers will send out your handsaws and circular-saw blades for sharpening, although they rarely do sharpening in-store.

## QUICK GLOSSARY

**CROSSCUT:** Cutting across the grain of the workpiece, straight or at an angle
**RIP:** Cutting with the grain

*Start a cut with a crosscut saw by lining up the blade and drawing the tool up to score the wood, far left. The score keeps the blade aligned during the first push, or cutting stroke. Near the end of the cut, hold the blade more vertically and support the waste piece with your hand to prevent tear-out.*

*The handy saber saw—also called a jigsaw—has a small, thin blade that is ideal for cutting curves. With different blades, a saber saw will cut plywood, plastics, metal, and other materials.*

# POWER SAWS

Power saws intended for home use are powerful, accurate, and affordable. They are a great aid to the finish carpenter, and help ensure that the work is completed efficiently.

## POWER MITER SAW

A power miter saw, sometimes called a chop saw, is one of the most useful tools of the finish carpenter. The most common type has a 10-inch-diameter blade and will cut stock up to 5 inches wide and 4 inches thick. A power miter saw has a bed and a fence that are aligned perfectly square to each other so the workpiece can be accurately positioned. The blade swivels to cut at a variety of angles—usually 45 degrees each side of center. In relationship to the bed of the tool, the blade stays fixed at 90 degrees. Most power miters have positive stops that can be engaged so that the blade will snap exactly into position to make 90- and 45-degree cuts. The best models have microadjustments so the stops can be tuned exactly—an excellent feature that helps produce fine joinery. For best results, equip your saw with a high-quality, 60- or 80-tooth, carbide-tipped blade, available at home improvement centers.

A close relative of the power miter saw is the power compound miter saw. This tool features a blade that both swivels and tilts. It is designed to cut complex compound miter joints—those with both a bevel and a miter. An example is a piece of crown molding that changes direction to follow the line of a ceiling up a stairway. These saws are more expensive than power miter saws.

Power miter saws are especially good for shaving the ends of a workpiece to make precise fits. With experience, you can shave less than $\frac{1}{32}$ of an inch from the end of a piece of molding. The trick is to set the workpiece snugly in the miter box, holding it firmly against the bed and fence. With your finger off the trigger, lower the blade of the tool until it just touches the workpiece. Nudge the workpiece and use the blade of the tool to judge how much you're going to shave. A full blade width is about $\frac{1}{8}$ inch. Half the blade's width is about $\frac{1}{16}$ inch. With the proper amount of the workpiece under the blade, raise the blade fully before pulling the trigger. Bring the blade down smoothly and easily, making sure you lower the blade fully. Release the trigger, and let the blade come to a complete stop before raising the blade and removing the piece.

*The power miter saw is one of the most useful power tools for finish carpentry. Use it to make angled cuts in moldings and trims. A compound miter saw, such as the one shown at right, makes complex cuts, such as miters in crown moldings. A built-in clamp helps hold the workpiece.*

## PRO ADVICE: DON'T CHOP A CHOP SAW

Contrary to its nickname—chop saw—you don't use a swift chopping motion when cutting with a power miter saw. Hold the workpiece firmly against both the bed and the fence, making sure your hands are completely out of the way of the blade. Use a block of wood the same height as the bed of the tool for additional support when cutting long workpieces. Bring the blade down with a smooth, firm action, cutting all the way through the workpiece. If you bring the blade down too fast, you might bind the blade or jolt the tool, with possibly disastrous results for your workpiece or your fingers.

## PRO ADVICE: BEWARE OF SMALL PIECES

When a cut will result in a waste piece an inch long or less, don't make the cut on a power miter saw. The motion of the spinning blade generates a little breeze that will easily pick up a small piece of wood. Often, these small pieces get sucked up into the safety housing and jam the blade. Worse, they can hit the blade and explode, sending splinters in all directions. Don't risk it; instead, use a handsaw.

*To make a straight rip cut with a circular saw, securely clamp a straightedge to the workpiece. Align the straightedge with care so that the saw cuts exactly along your cutting line. Test the setup on a piece of scrap, then measure the distance from the straightedge to the saw kerf.*

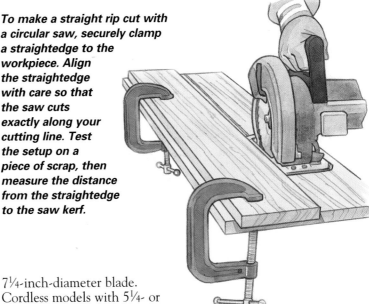

### SABER SAW

A saber saw, sometimes called a jigsaw or a bayonet saw, is a versatile, all-purpose cutting tool that is especially useful for cutting curves. It has a thin blade that cuts with an up-and-down stroke. Blades are interchangeable, and a saber saw can be equipped with blades made especially for cutting wood, metal, plastics, or plywood. It can make straight crosscuts or rip cuts. Run the foot of the tool along an edge guide to make precise straight cuts. Some models have a tilting base for cutting angles; these saws could make compound miter cuts.

### CIRCULAR SAW

A circular saw is best for cutting framing lumber and sheet goods. In finish carpentry, its use is limited to cutting shelving or ripping large stock. To obtain a reliably straight edge, run the saw along an edge guide, as shown above right. The standard circular saw has a 7¼-inch-diameter blade. Cordless models with 5¼- or 6-inch blades are becoming more popular for trim work.

### TABLE SAW

A table saw allows you to make safe, accurate cuts. You can set the saw's movable fence to rip a workpiece to precise width—even a long, thin piece of wood. The table saw's sliding miter gauge helps cut accurate crosscuts or, if you also tilt the saw's blade, compound miter cuts. Cutting on a table saw calls for constant attention and caution because the operator exerts force toward the spinning blade. For safety, guide the workpiece past the blade with push sticks, keeping hands and fingers well out of the way, as shown below.

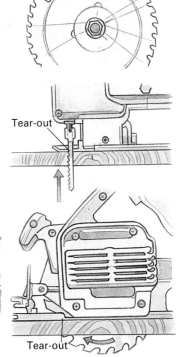

Tear-out

Tear-out

Tear-out

*The direction the teeth move determines which side of the workpiece will have small splinters or tear-out. For a table saw, (top), it's the bottom of the workpiece; for the saber saw and circular saw, the tear-out occurs on the top of the workpiece.*

*Keep fingers away from your table-saw blade by using a push stick. A feather board, made by sawing a series of parallel kerfs in the end of a board, applies gentle but firm pressure to ensure that a workpiece stays against the table-saw fence.*

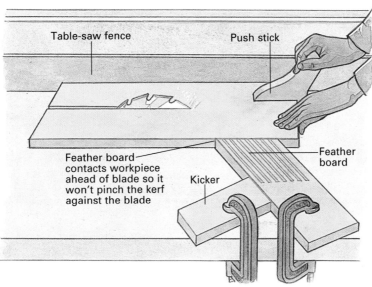

Table-saw fence

Push stick

Feather board contacts workpiece ahead of blade so it won't pinch the kerf against the blade

Kicker

Feather board

*A router is ideal for shaping wood for joinery such as a dovetail.*

# ROUTERS

Routers and router bits cut shapes in wood or trim the edges of wood and other materials, such as plastic laminates. The bit turns at extremely high speed, resulting in clean and precise cuts. Routers are especially useful for cutting grooves to make joinery, such as the dadoes used to support the shelves of a built-in bookcase. A 1- or 1½-horsepower motor is adequate for general use. Use a router rated at 2 or 3 horsepower for especially rigorous jobs, such as making your own moldings from hardwood.

Router bits come in dozens of shapes. For long life and reliable sharpness, choose carbide-tipped bits. Any bit for shaping the edges of stock should have a guide bearing, sometimes called a pilot bearing. This tiny ball bearing guides the bit along the edge of the workpiece,

maintaining the correct cutting depth. A solid guide tip, found on less-expensive bits, spins at the same high speed as the bit itself, making it liable to scorch and mar the edge of the workpiece.

Routers are hand-held tools. However, router tables are available that allow you to mount the tool upside down, with the cutting bit protruding through a hole in the work surface. A fence guides the stock against the bit. This is a safe way to work with a router. It also permits precise alignment of cuts, such as shallow grooves or flutes, that are to be made in the middle of a piece of stock. The fireplace mantel shown on pages 82–85 features flutes in the pilasters cut with a table-mounted router.

Plunge routers are another type of router. The plunge router can be set up so that the body moves freely up and down on guide shafts. By positioning the tool over a workpiece and lowering the bit into the stock, a plunge router cuts into the middle of a workpiece without the need to drill a starter hole. An example of this technique is when using a router to cut a hole for a sink in the middle of a countertop. A plunge router has limited uses in finish carpentry. However, it is possible to fix the body of a plunge router in one position so that the tool can be used as a conventional router. If you use a router for a variety of woodworking tasks, consider the versatility of a plunge router.

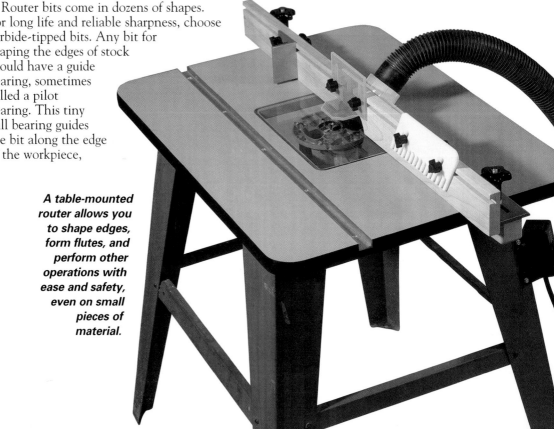

*A table-mounted router allows you to shape edges, form flutes, and perform other operations with ease and safety, even on small pieces of material.*

**TABLE-MOUNTED ROUTER**

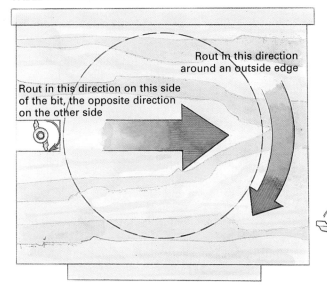

Rout in this direction around an outside edge

Rout in this direction on this side of the bit, the opposite direction on the other side

**HANDHELD ROUTER**

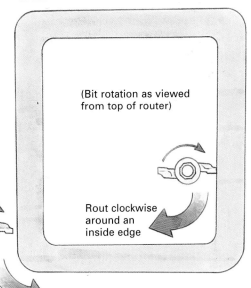

(Bit rotation as viewed from top of router)

Rout clockwise around an inside edge

Rout counterclockwise around an outside edge

*When shaping with a handheld router, always move the tool clockwise on inside edges, counterclockwise on outside edges.*

The direction of bit rotation—clockwise when looking down on the router from its top—determines which way you move the tool on the workpiece. Because the bit turns at such high speed, it should move along the workpiece so the cutting edge is rotating into the material, as shown above right. If you were to move the router in the direction of the spin, this powerful tool could easily pull itself right out of your hands. If possible, try to position yourself so that you pull the router toward you, rather than pushing it away. When routing the outside edge of a workpiece, move the router in a counterclockwise direction. When routing the inside edge, the tool is moved clockwise.

A router bit spins fast enough to prevent most tear-out of a wood workpiece, even when operating against the direction of the grain. However, for deep or complex cuts, it's a good idea to make a series of progressively deeper cuts until you get the desired profile. Also, if you are cutting against the grain at the end of a workpiece, tear-out is likely. Prevent damage to the workpiece by cutting it longer than necessary, then trimming it to length after routing is complete. Or, clamp a scrap block of wood securely to the end of the workpiece and extend the router cut into the scrap.

### PRO ADVICE: HANG ON TIGHT!

**CAUTION!** When you turn on a router, it comes up to full speed almost immediately. This sudden twisting force is called torque, and a router can develop quite a bit of it. Always keep a firm grip on your router when starting the tool to prevent it from twisting out of your hands.

*Router bits come in many shapes to cut decorative edges and produce smooth, precise grooves and rabbets that are used in joinery. The best blades have carbide cutters for long life and roller guide tips to prevent the blade from scorching the workpiece.*

# CHISELS

A chisel is one of the most useful tools for the finish carpenter. It cuts grooves, removes waste stock, and shaves away small slivers of material that make all the difference between an adequate job and a superior one.

The key to a chisel's utility is its sharpness. Keep chisels in top condition by sharpening them on a sharpening stone. You can master the technique with a little practice. The same techniques also keep hand plane blades sharp (see pages 30–31).

There are different types of chisels—paring, firmer, butt, pocket, framer's, and bench. The differences are subtle—some have beveled sides, and some feature especially long blades. For finish carpentry, you can rely on utility and woodworker's chisels. A utility chisel has an impact-resistant plastic handle with a metal strike plate. The steel blade tang of some types goes all the way through the handle to form the strike plate. A woodworker's chisel has a handle of wood or molded plastic. The handle is contoured

to fit in the hand comfortably, and the tool is driven by hand pressure rather than by a hammer or mallet. Never strike a chisel with a hammer unless it has a metal strike plate.

When selecting a chisel, choose a style that feels comfortable. A chisel with a ¾-inch-wide blade is a good all-purpose size. For a second chisel, consider a narrow, ¼-inch-wide blade for getting into tight spaces. It's tempting to think that an expensive chisel offers superior quality, but if the blade is kept sharp and free of nicks, any chisel will provide satisfactory results. If your chisel dulls too easily, try another brand or style to see if the different steel holds an edge better.

## USING CHISELS

The best way to use a chisel is to push it by hand with firm, even pressure. A sharp blade will cut material easily. To shave a lot of material, lay the chisel flat, with the bevel side up. If it's not possible to lay the chisel flat, place the bevel side down so the chisel point will not be driven into the wood.

Use a chisel to shave an uneven joint so that the surfaces are flush. To do this, work from the high side toward the low one, shaving away wood until the surfaces are even. Cut with the grain. Work with the back of the chisel flat against the workpiece.

When making vertical cuts, the workpiece must be firmly clamped. Outline the cut with the edge of the chisel, holding the beveled side of the chisel toward the waste. Tap the end of the chisel with a mallet to cut into the surface of the workpiece, working around the entire outline of the cut. Drive the chisel progressively deeper until the desired depth is reached. To prevent tear-out when shaving end grain, place a scrap piece of wood under the workpiece.

*Hollow Grinding a Chisel:* Hollow-grind the cutting bevel on a bench grinder. Don't hold the chisel against the wheel for more than a few seconds at a time or the temper of the steel will be ruined. Give the blade 15 seconds to cool off between passes.

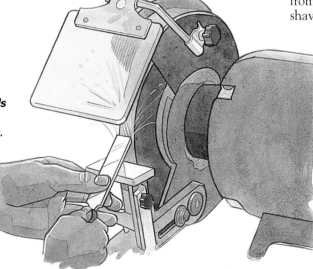

## SHARPENING CHISELS

You can sharpen a chisel on a flat stone, as shown below, or on a bench grinder, as shown on the opposite page. The sharpening process using a bench grinder is called hollow grinding. It imparts a slightly concave shape to the bevel. When placed on a bench stone for final sharpening, only the tip and heel of a hollow-ground bevel come in contact with the stone, making it much easier to put a razor-sharp edge on the cutting edge. A hollow-ground tool retains its concave shape for many sharpenings on the bench stone, making it possible to quickly touch up an edge and restore sharpness.

Equip your bench grinder with a 60-grit silicon carbide or aluminum oxide wheel. The grinder should have a tool rest to position your chisel (or plane blade) at the proper angle for grinding—about 25 degrees.

After repeated use, a grinding wheel will become unevenly worn and clogged with grit, bits of steel, and other residue. When this happens, dressing will clean the surface of the wheel, restore a square edge, and restore the wheel's roundness. A star dressing wheel or an abrasive stick, available at most hardware stores or home improvement centers that sell

grinding wheels, will do the job. The dressing tool is applied to the grinding wheel while it is spinning and will restore the wheel to peak condition in a few minutes.

Finish the sharpening job with a bench stone. Both water stones and oil stones require a lubricant to allow the tool to move smoothly over the surface of the stone and to carry away waste particles. A water stone should be well-saturated with water; an oil stone uses a few drops of lightweight machine oil. Both types of stones work well. Look for a combination stone that features a coarse grit on one side and a fine grit on the other. Diamond stones and natural sharpening stones are also available, but these are usually expensive and are used mostly by professional woodworkers.

### PRO ADVICE: PROTECT CHISEL EDGES

Protect the blade of a chisel when not in use by laying it with the bevel side down. That way, the cutting edge is lifted slightly off the surrounding surfaces. Never drop a chisel into a nail bag— the cutting edge is sure to be nicked by nails or screws. To store a chisel, use a chisel guard or wrap it in an old piece of leather to protect it and keep it sharp.

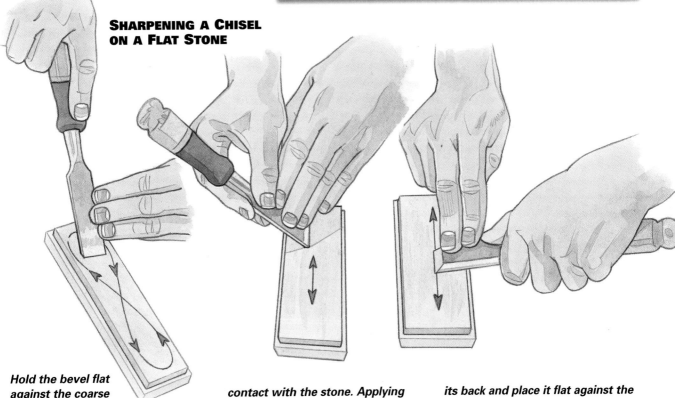

**SHARPENING A CHISEL ON A FLAT STONE**

*Hold the bevel flat against the coarse side of a properly lubricated combination bench stone. Make sure both the heel and toe of the bevel are in contact with the stone. Applying firm, even pressure, move the tool in a figure-eight pattern. It will develop a thin piece of excess metal at the tip—the "wire edge." Flip the tool on its back and place it flat against the stone. Slowly draw the chisel from side to side using light pressure to remove the wire edge. Turn the stone over and repeat the process.*

# SANDERS

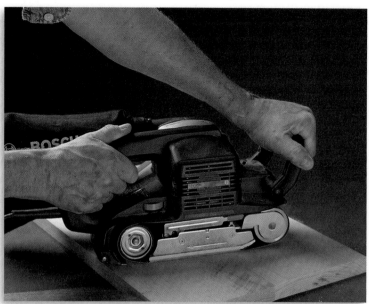

*A belt sander can remove a lot of stock quickly, especially when positioned to sand across the grain as shown. Use a firm, two-handed grip and apply even pressure on the sanding plate.*

Most dimensional lumber, molding, and trim has imperfections such as small knotholes, splintered edges, gouges, and planer marks—the small wavy undulations caused by dull or out-of-alignment planer blades used at large production mills. These imperfections should be sanded out of workpieces before installation. Small blemishes are easily detected in finish work—even under several coats of paint.

The finish carpenter should have two sanders—a belt sander for fast removal and smoothing of material, and a palm sander for fine detail work and spot sanding. When sanding complex shapes, such as intricate molding, you'll probably need to sand the old-fashioned way—by hand. However, new electric detail sanders have removable sanding heads of various shapes that smooth small curves, grooves, and other hard-to-reach areas. If your finish carpentry project requires lots of fine sanding, you may want to purchase an electric detail sander.

## BELT SANDERS

A belt sander uses a strong electric motor to run a continuous loop of sandpaper—a belt—over a flat sanding plate at high speed. The tool is rated by the size of its belt. A 3×21 sander uses a belt 3 inches wide and 21 inches in circumference and is a good choice for home use. A 4×24 sander often is used by professional cabinet and furniture makers. Sanding belts come in various grits and should be used in progression from coarse to fine. Select a model with an attached bag that collects dust.

A belt sander is a powerful tool that can remove a lot of wood in a short time. Take care not to damage the workpiece. Clamp the stock firmly in place or the friction of the belt will grab the piece and literally shoot it across the room. Grip the sander firmly and apply even pressure to the sanding plate, but don't push so hard that the tool slows down noticeably. Keep the sander moving to prevent removing too much from one area, and don't rock the tool at the end of the workpiece or you'll risk rounding over the square edge. Sanding across the grain leaves deep scratches in the wood; for finish work, sand with the grain and use short, overlapping strokes to cover the entire workpiece.

*A palm sander smooths wood and removes minor scratches and marks. Most palm sanders have dust-collection bags. Sanders with hook-and-loop-type pads allow paper to be changed quickly and easily.*

*With different pads, this contour sander can sand coves, beads, and other curves in moldings. You'll also find detail sanders, with oscillating triangular sanding pads, that allow you to sand into corners.*

## PALM SANDERS

Palm sanders, sometimes called random-orbit sanders, are smaller and easier to control than belt sanders. They are used to smooth smaller amounts of surface material or to put the final touch on a workpiece. The square or circular sanding pad at the bottom of the sander vibrates rapidly and moves in many directions, so the tool doesn't have to move with the grain. However, it's always a good idea to sand with the grain when using coarse-grit sandpapers. Palm sanders are designed to be used with one hand, freeing the other hand to steady the workpiece. Some models have dust bags.

*Hand sanding is efficient and sometimes necessary to smooth odd shapes or areas that are hard to reach with an electric sander. With some ingenuity, you can create sanding blocks of various shapes. Use a paint roller with a short nap to hold sandpaper when sanding curved cutouts. Make a detail sander from scrap wood. Buy adhesive-backed sandpaper and cut it to fit the sanding pad.*

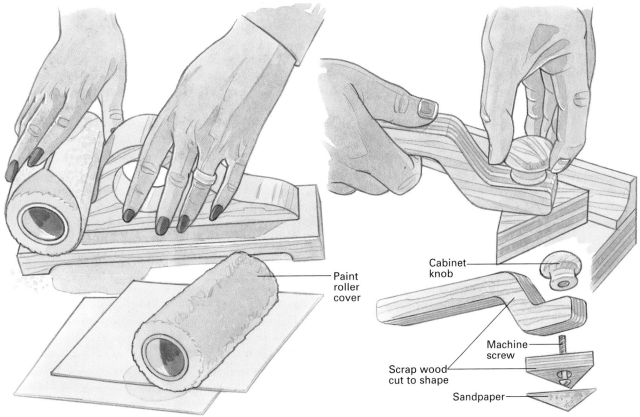

Paint roller cover

Cabinet knob

Machine screw

Scrap wood cut to shape

Sandpaper

# PLANES, RASPS, AND FILES

Shaping tool

Rasp

## PLANES

Use a hand plane to quickly shave excess wood from lumber or millwork and to smooth the surface of rough or damaged boards. Planing with a sharp blade removes paper-thin shavings without creating dust and is the preferred way to trim long, narrow edges or to straighten slightly warped or twisted boards. A 10- to 12-inch-long smoothing plane, sometimes called a jack or bench plane, is a good all-purpose plane. A 6- to 7-inch-long block plane with a blade set at a low angle is ideal for cutting across the end grain of a piece of wood. Use a block plane for trimming miters or relieving the back of a piece of molding to make close-fitting joints.

The blade of a plane is covered with an adjustable cap iron—a flat piece of steel with a rolled tip that is designed to limit the amount of cutting edge available. It also deflects the waste shavings up and out of the mouth of the tool. The position of the cap iron on the blade helps determine how deep the blade will cut. The closer the cap iron is to the tip of the blade, the finer the cut will be. The depth of the cut can also be set by turning the knurled adjustment knob at the back of the tool, extending the blade and cap iron assembly farther through the throat or retracting it.

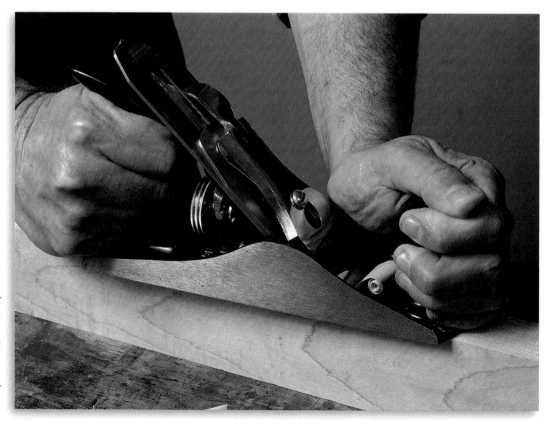

*A jack or bench plane with a 10- to 12-inch-long body is especially useful for smoothing the edges of boards. Use a firm, two-handed grip and keep even pressure on the heel and toe of the tool.*

The key to good results is to keep the plane blade sharp. Use the techniques for sharpening chisel blades described on page 27. However, it's more difficult to hold a wide, thin plane blade flat against the surface of a stone without rocking slightly from side to side. To keep from rocking a plane blade, use a honing guide. A honing guide locks the blade into position for sharpening and rolls along the stone on small wheels.

## FILES AND RASPS

Files remove and shape wood, metal, and plastic. Rasps are used only on wood. The teeth of a file are actually a series of grooves cut into the metal. A single-cut file has one set of parallel grooves. A double-cut file has two sets that cross each other to form diamond patterns. Rasps have coarse, individually shaped teeth that remove large amounts of wood quickly. Both come in various degrees of coarseness.

Files have many profiles—flat, round, half-round, triangular, square, and oval. For the finish carpenter, files are specialty tools that are handy for trimming or shaping hard-to-reach spots or complex molding designs in wood or plastic. They are ideal for shaving cutouts in plastic laminate flooring (see pages 52–55). Because they smooth only a small, defined area at a time, files require less pressure than sandpaper and are good for delicate tasks, such as shaping a coped joint to make a perfect fit. Keep files in top working order by using a file card to clean the teeth regularly. A file card is a small paddle with stiff metal bristles on one side for removing built-up metal shavings, and softer nylon bristles on the other for removing built-up wood or plastic.

The most common rasps are flat, round, or half-round. Serrated rasps have plastic or metal bodies with removable blades that are easily replaced when dull. Rasps are useful for reshaping and adjusting out-of-align framing materials, or for removing excess wallboard from around window or door frames so that casing can be installed flush to the surrounding surfaces.

*To prevent the wood from tearing, always move a hand plane in the direction of the wood grain, also known as the lift of the grain. Adjust the blade depth so that the shavings are about the thickness of heavy paper.*

*A block plane is useful for cutting the end grain of wood. To prevent tear-out, clamp a scrap block of wood flush with the workpiece. Make sure the blade is sharp.*

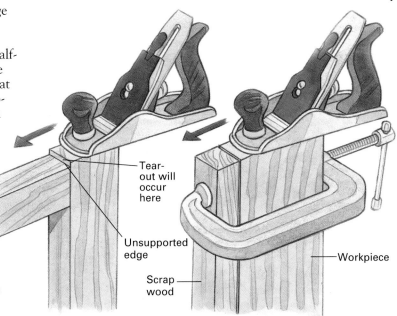

Tear-out will occur here

Unsupported edge

Scrap wood

Workpiece

## PRO ADVICE: CARING FOR PLANES

When storing a plane, always protect the blade from nicks to keep it from becoming dull. If you won't be using the plane for long periods, retract the blade fully before placing it on the shelf.

# HAMMERS

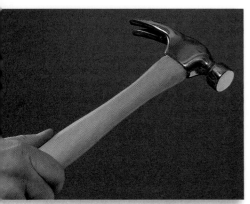
*Claw Hammer*

*Wooden Mallet*

*Dead-blow hammer*

*Cross-peen hammer*

This fundamental carpenter's tool is available in many styles, shapes, and weights, each intended for various tasks. When purchasing a hammer, one of your first considerations should be comfort; having a hammer that feels well-balanced helps ensure accurate swings and years of satisfaction.

A finish carpenter needs at least two hammers: a medium-weight hammer for general use, and a lightweight hammer for more delicate tasks, such as driving small finish nails and brads. Select a hammer with a 16-ounce head for general use, and a 10- or 13-ounce hammer for lightweight jobs. For more robust work, such as driving 16d nails into framing lumber, choose a heavier 20- to 28-ounce framing hammer.

Carpenter's hammers have two types of heads—curved claw and straight claw. The curved claw head is sometimes called a cabinetmaker's hammer. It is intended for use in tight spaces, such as working inside a piece of furniture. The straight claw, sometimes called a ripping claw, offers better power when pulling nails, and the claw is easier to manipulate when prying materials apart.

Choose a hammer that feels balanced when you swing it with an easy arm motion. The heads of most medium and lightweight hammers have a striking face with a smooth surface. Larger framing hammers often have a scored face to prevent the head from slipping off a nail if the

blow is slightly askew. This is a good reason not to use a framing hammer for finish tasks. If you miss a nail, the dent you'll create in the surrounding material is made even more difficult to repair by the crosshatch pattern of the head.

## HAMMER HANDLES

Hammer handles are made of wood, fiberglass, or steel. All make good hammers. Wood has the ability to absorb the shock of repeated blows. Its main drawback is a tendency to crack when extreme force is exerted, such as when pulling a stubborn nail or prying apart materials. For that reason, use wood-handled hammers only for driving nails. Wood handles can be replaced, and new handles are readily available at hardware stores and home improvement centers.

Fiberglass-handled hammers offer resiliency and toughness. They absorb shock well and are nearly unbreakable. A hammer with a fiberglass handle is often the longest-lived tool in the carpenter's toolbox.

Steel handles are either solid or tubular. Hammers with solid steel handles are the toughest of all hammers—some framing carpenters regularly use them as prying tools and for demolition work. Handles of tubular steel have better resiliency and concentrate more of the hammer's overall weight at the head, making it easier to swing with accuracy. They are strong, but not as strong as solid steel.

Hammers with steel or fiberglass handles usually have cushion grips that help absorb shock and make the tool more comfortable to hold.

## MALLETS

A mallet is a specialty tool used for striking other tools, such as chisels, that may require a forceful blow to cut wood or other materials. Mallets are characterized by large heads made of wood or dense rubber that absorb shock to prevent damage to the tool they are striking. A good example is using a mallet to drive a wood-handled chisel. Mallets also are valuable for tapping workpieces into alignment without risking damage to the surface or edge. Mallets with wooden heads are popular among serious woodworkers and will not mar workpieces that they contact. A dead-blow hammer has a nonmetallic face and strikes without rebound, which minimizes denting. It's a good choice for aligning parts. A rubber-headed mallet won't dent most woods, but the black rubber head may leave

Nail sets

black marks on the workpiece that are difficult to remove. White-headed mallets may leave white marks.

## USING AN AIR NAILER

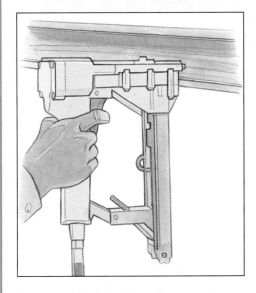

Air nailers, sometimes called pneumatic nailers, use compressed air to shoot nails into workpieces. The system includes a nailing gun, a flexible air hose, and an air compressor. Although the setup is expensive, you can rent the entire system at most rental stores.

The pressure used to drive the nails is adjustable, making it possible to tune the tool so that nails are countersunk a precise distance below the surface of the workpiece. Nail guns make short work of nailing up trim and molding and offer several advantages over hand nailing:

■ The gun can be operated with one hand, leaving the other hand free to steady the trim and keep it aligned.

■ A single blow drives the nail from an air gun, not repeated hammer blows that may tend to jolt a piece out of alignment.

■ There is no risk of bending a nail or missing the nailhead and damaging the workpiece.

■ Nails used in nail guns have blunt tips that help prevent splitting the workpiece.

## NAIL SETS

A nail set is a small tapered piece of steel used to drive finish nails below the surface of the workpiece. The tips are made in various diameters to match nails of different diameters. You should have a $\frac{1}{32}$, a $\frac{2}{32}$ ($\frac{1}{16}$), and a $\frac{3}{32}$ set. When using a nail set, the shaft of the set should be perfectly in line with the nail so that the force of the hammer blow is transferred directly to the nail. If the set is not aligned properly, it will slip off the nailhead when struck.

**PROTECTING MOLDING FROM HAMMER DENTS**

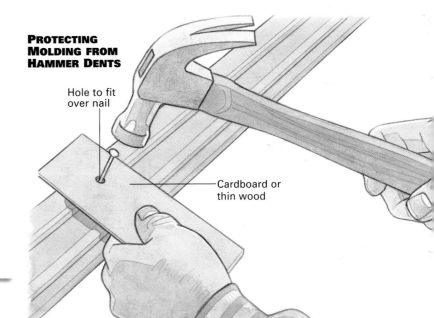

Hole to fit over nail

Cardboard or thin wood

# DRILLS AND SCREWDRIVERS

Use drills to make pilot holes, to create countersink holes for screws, to fashion plugs for hiding screw heads, to make holes of all sizes in virtually any material, and to drive screws.

With so many accessories available, the power drill is one of the most popular tools

*A brace and auger bit, like these vintage tools, still come in handy for some jobs today. Electric drills, either corded or cordless, have largely replaced hand drills like this crank-operated one.*

of professional carpenters and homeowners. Power drills are either corded or cordless. Corded drills must be plugged in to an electrical outlet. Their advantage is superior power and the availability of a constant, reliable source of electricity needed to operate the tool. Cordless models are battery-operated. Their advantage is

portability and convenience. The batteries that run these tools must be periodically recharged. With moderate (not continual) use, a drill battery will last 2 to 3 hours between charges.

Look for a power drill that has variable speeds, a keyless chuck, an adjustable clutch for screw driving, and an electric brake. A ⅜-inch chuck is standard, but some drills have a ½-inch chuck, which permits the use of larger bits. A variable-speed drill allows you to control the speed at which the chuck turns by varying the pressure of your finger on the trigger. An electric brake stops the chuck the instant you release the trigger—a good safety feature. Most name-brand drills are well built and backed by good warranties; concentrate on selecting one that is comfortable in your hand and feels well balanced.

For cordless drills, choose a 12-volt or 14.4-volt model. These have adequate power with moderate weight. Bigger drills, such as 18- and 24-volt models, offer more power but are too heavy for finish carpentry. Purchase a second battery so you can have one on the charger while the other is in use.

## HAND DRILLS

Although cordless tools are popular, the original hand-operated cordless tools are still readily available today. Hand drills—the crank-operated hand drill, bit brace, and push drill—are reliable, easy to use, and portable. A hand drill with a sharp bit often will drill a hole nearly as fast as a power drill.

Crank-operated drills are good for general finish work. Select a model that has two gears—not just one—that support the crank wheel. A brace, sometimes called a ratchet brace, can bore larger holes with auger bits. You can also fit one with a bit for driving screws; a brace with a screwdriver bit can

## USING A COUNTERSINK BIT

Use a countersink bit to hide the head of a screw below the surface of a workpiece. The size of the countersink bit is matched to the size of the screw, so the hole is always a perfect fit. The bit leaves a smooth hole with a standard diameter that can be plugged with a piece of wood cut with a plug cutter. For finish-grade work, use a plug cutter and make plugs from the same type of wood as the workpiece to camouflage the screw location.

generate as much torque as many electric drills. Push-type drills have a spring-powered mechanism. Pushing up and down on the handle of the drill compresses and releases the spring, turning the shaft. Push-type drills can be used for drilling holes or turning screws. They are easily carried in a tool belt or a nail apron and are a handy accessory for the finish carpenter.

## DRILL BITS AND ACCESSORIES

Drill bits come in many shapes and sizes. If sharp, most drill bits perform well. For finish carpentry work, you should have a set of twist drills with either conical tips or brad points. Brad-point bits feature a small, sharp spur in the center of the bit to keep it steady and on target as you begin to drill. Many new twist drill designs have pilot tips for easier and truer starting. To keep conical-tip drills from wandering, first dent the center of the hole location with an awl. Your drilling accessories should also include a set of screw tips for driving screws. Have tips for driving phillips, flat-blade, and square-drive screws. Purchase different size tips of each variety to fit screws of different sizes.

*The combination screwdriver uses interchangeable tips to fit most common screws.*

## SCREWDRIVERS

Screwdrivers are probably the most misused tools of all time. These handy items are often employed as pry bars, chisels, demolition tools, and scrapers. For the most part, screwdrivers are tough enough to stand abuse. However, proper use ensures a long life for the tool, and will prevent damage to screw heads.

A screwdriver with a broken, twisted, or worn tip will damage the head of a screw, making it difficult, if not impossible, to drive in or remove after the damage is done.

Handles of screwdrivers typically are made of tough polypropylene, and shafts are either square or round steel. You'll need a set of screwdrivers to handle various types of screw head configurations—slotted, phillips, and square drive. A combination screwdriver features interchangeable tips that are stored within the shaft or the handle of the tool. A well-made combination screwdriver provides two sizes of slotted blade tips and two phillips head tips, all in one screwdriver.

*Twist drills and screwdriver bits are the drill accessories you'll use most often. A magnetic bit holder simplifies driving screws.*

### PRO ADVICE: PICKING A BIT

When selecting a bit to drill a pilot hole for nails, choose one with a slightly smaller diameter than the nail you'll drive. Although you want to clean out material to prevent splitting the wood, the hole should be slightly smaller than the diameter of the nail shaft so that the shaft—in addition to the nailhead—provides some holding power. If you have trouble estimating the difference for small nails, use a caliper to measure the shank of the nail, then choose a bit that is $1/64$ inch smaller.

When selecting a drill bit to make a pilot hole for a screw, choose a bit that has the same diameter as the screw shaft, minus the threads. Hold the screw and the bit up to a light together to make sure the bit is properly sized.

# CLAMPS

*The C-clamp, bar clamp, spring clamp, and speed clamp are essentials for finish carpentry.*

Clamps can hold workpieces securely for maximum control and safety while cutting, sanding, shaping, or adding fasteners. Clamps also draw pieces together and hold them in position for gluing. You'll find many shapes and sizes of clamps, each offering certain advantages for different clamping tasks. Here are some clamps that will help in finish carpentry:

**C-CLAMP:** Instantly recognizable by its C-shaped body, this general-purpose clamp can apply lots of pressure, thanks to its rigidity and strength. C-clamps use a long, threaded steel screw to apply clamping force; the body is made of steel, aluminum, or iron. They are good for securing workpieces to a bench top.

**SPRING CLAMP:** These small holding devices generate clamping force from powerful springs—no further tightening

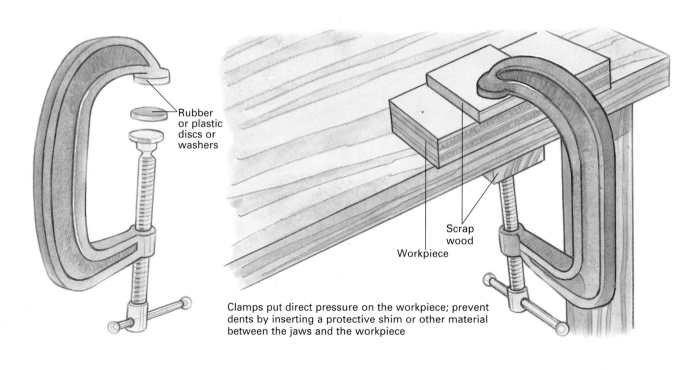

Rubber or plastic discs or washers

Scrap wood

Workpiece

Clamps put direct pressure on the workpiece; prevent dents by inserting a protective shim or other material between the jaws and the workpiece is necessary. Spring clamps are designed to be operated by one hand and can be positioned quickly and easily.

**BAR AND PIPE CLAMP:** These are designed for wide clamping jobs, such as edge-joining two or more wide boards. The system features a movable jaw on one end that is positioned by hand. Once released, a self-locking mechanism keeps it firmly in place. The other end is fixed but has an adjustable jaw that is tightened by a screw. Bar clamps are made as a unit and the rigid bar helps keep the jaws in alignment. Pipe clamps come as just the two stops. You must purchase a length of ½-inch or ¾-inch black iron plumbing pipe to make the finished clamp. After the pipe is cut to length, one end is threaded to receive the fixed stop. The pipe can be cut to any length to create inexpensive custom clamps. A disadvantage is that with repeated use, the pipe may become slightly bent and need to be replaced.

**SPEED CLAMP:** Variations on the bar clamp, these have a thumb-operated latch that allows the jaw to slide so it can be quickly closed on the workpiece. When squeezed, the pistol-type trigger applies the clamping pressure. A speed clamp can be operated by one hand, leaving the other hand free to steady the workpieces.

**HAND SCREW:** The traditional favorite of fine woodworkers, a hand screw has two large wooden jaws that are opened and closed by two parallel screws. Operating the clamp correctly takes some practice. Once mastered, however, the hand screw is an excellent helpmate. It has lots of holding power, it is easily positioned, and the wooden jaws will not mar the workpiece, making protective shims unnecessary. The jaws can be positioned at odd angles to hold or join irregularly shaped workpieces.

**VISE:** A vise is a clamp permanently attached to a workbench. One jaw is fixed and the other is operated by turning a threaded shaft with a handle. To avoid having to screw the jaws together, some vises have quick-release jaws that slide back and forth easily. Vises typically have big jaws with lots of holding power; workpieces should be protected with shims. Vises are especially

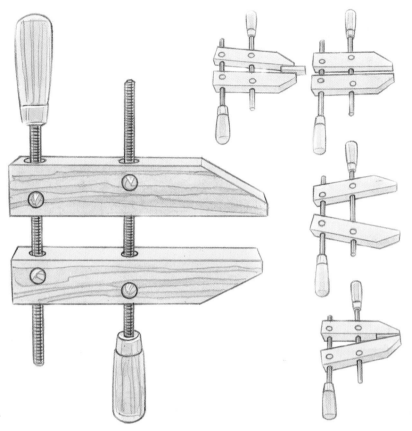

*The hand screw's independently adjustable jaws adapt to fit most clamping challenges.*

good for holding long workpieces for planing, sanding, or doweling. Work close to the vise to ensure that the workpiece remains rigid. Working too far from a vise or clamp risks flexing the workpiece, causing tools to accidentally slip.

### PRO ADVICE: ALIGNMENT CHECK

When using clamps to glue up two pieces of stock, take time to ensure that the surfaces are properly aligned before applying final pressure. Some carpenters use clamps to snug the joints together, then tap the piece into final alignment with a hammer or mallet before applying final pressure. When edge-joining wide boards, use a level or the long edge of a framing square to ensure that the surface formed by the boards is flat. If it isn't, release the clamping pressure and realign the boards.

# BASIC JOINERY

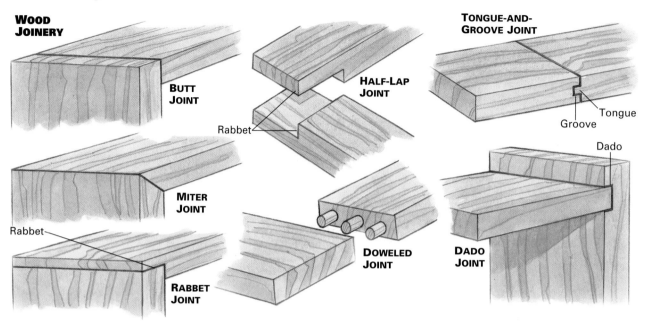

**WOOD JOINERY**

**BUTT JOINT**

**HALF-LAP JOINT**

Rabbet

**TONGUE-AND-GROOVE JOINT**

Tongue

Groove

Dado

**MITER JOINT**

Rabbet

**RABBET JOINT**

**DOWELED JOINT**

**DADO JOINT**

*Use basic joinery to fasten two pieces of wood together. Most basic joints require both glue and mechanical fasteners—either nails or screws—to hold the workpieces securely. The doweled joint retains its strength with only glue.*

The technique used to fasten two pieces of wood together is called joinery. Mastering a few simple joints is important for achieving good-looking results with finish carpentry projects. The key to good joinery is making clean, accurate cuts. Sharp tools and precise measurements will result in joints that fit together without gaps.

**BUTT JOINT:** In a butt joint, the end of one piece of wood meets the face of another, typically at a right angle. A butt joint has no inherent strength, so a mechanical fastener, such as a nail or screw, is needed. Glue alone will not make a strong butt joint. For a good butt joint, saw the end of the butted piece perfectly square, not only across the face of the wood but across its thickness as well. Make cuts for a butt joint with a miter saw or table saw.

## USING A BISCUIT JOINER

A biscuit joiner (shown on opposite page) makes exceptionally strong joints. It has a circular cutter head that makes matching, arc-shaped slots in the materials to be joined. Once the slots are cut, a flat, football-shaped piece of compressed wood—the biscuit—is coated with glue and inserted into the slots. The two workpieces are then clamped together while the glue dries. The key to the joint is the precise fit of the slot and the biscuit. The tool uses a rigid fence to make sure the two slots are cut exactly the same distance from the surface of the pieces. Once coated with glue, the biscuit begins to swell slightly, creating an extremely tight, strong joint.

**MITER JOINT:** The most common type of miter joint forms a right angle from pieces with ends cut at 45-degree angles. For any miter joint, the ends of the joined pieces are cut at identical angles. Miters are simple, clean, decorative joints commonly used for all types of moldings and trims. For strength, a mitered joint needs a mechanical fastener, dowels, or biscuits (see below left). Cut miters with a power miter saw or table saw.

**HALF-LAP JOINT:** This joint, for two pieces of the same thickness, is formed by removing half the thickness of each piece at the end. The width of each lap is determined by the width of the adjoining piece—the width of the joint made in piece A equals the width of board B, and vice versa. Half-laps form exceptionally strong corners. They can be reinforced with mechanical fasteners, but care must be taken to ensure that the fasteners do not crack the material or penetrate beyond the thickness of the joint. A half-lap joint is usually glued and clamped until the adhesive is thoroughly dry. Cut the half-lap with a table saw or router equipped with a straight bit. Make the shoulder cut—the innermost cut—first, using a guide. Then remove the remaining waste.

**LAP JOINT:** In this joint, a half-lapped piece fits into a dado in another—a half-lap joint that's not at the end of one piece. The depth of the dado equals the thickness of lap, and the width matches the width of the board being let in. This is stronger than a butt joint because the shoulder of the rabbet adds strength to the joint. You can add nails or screws in two directions for more strength.

## JOINERY CUTS

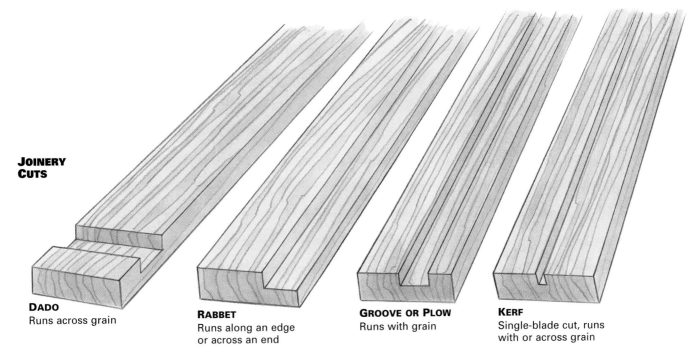

**DADO**
Runs across grain

**RABBET**
Runs along an edge
or across an end

**GROOVE OR PLOW**
Runs with grain

**KERF**
Single-blade cut, runs
with or across grain

**DADO JOINT:** A board is butted into a groove cut into another board to make a dado joint. Dado refers to both the type of joinery and to the groove itself. A dado is a three-sided channel, usually as deep as one-third to one-half the thickness of the board, running across the grain. Cut the dado using a router with a straight bit or a table saw equipped with a dado blade. A close-fitting dado joint is strong with either fasteners or glue, or both. To ensure a close fit, cut the dado in a scrap piece of wood and test the joint's fit. Then cut the finished piece.

**DOWELED JOINT:** Here wooden pins, called dowels, reinforce the joint. The difficulty lies in locating the dowel holes in each piece so that the surfaces of the joined pieces are perfectly flush. For drilling, use a doweling jig, which clamps onto the edge of the workpiece and centers a drill guide on it. The jig also ensures the drill bit enters the workpiece straight. A typical doweled joint in ¾-inch-thick material uses ⅜-inch-diameter dowels. When drilling, make sure the length of the dowel is ⅛ to ¼ inch less than the combined length of the holes. Mark the proper length on the drill bit with tape, and check the depth of the holes with the depth gauge of a caliper. For added strength, coat the dowel with white or yellow

polyvinyl acetate glue before insertion.

**TONGUE-AND-GROOVE JOINT:** This joint is most often used to join the edges of long pieces of material, such as flooring or wall paneling. Because the individual pieces are typically fastened to a solid substrate—a subfloor or battens—the joint itself does not need to be structural. For a structural joint along the length of two boards, use dowels or biscuits. (See Using a Biscuit Joiner on the opposite page.)

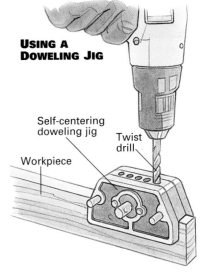

**USING A DOWELING JIG**

Self-centering
doweling jig
Twist
drill
Workpiece

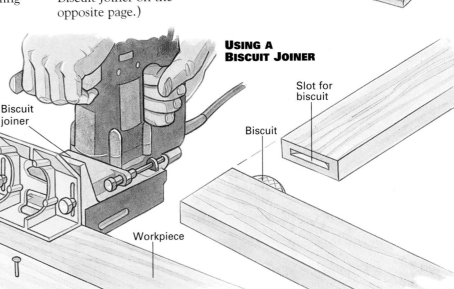

**USING A BISCUIT JOINER**

Biscuit
joiner

Cleat to press
workpiece
against

Workpiece

Slot for
biscuit

Biscuit

# TRIM JOINERY

Molding and trim work is basic joinery, such as miters and butt joints, done with care and precision. The key is patience; top-quality finish carpentry requires taking the time to do the job right.

Houses usually aren't perfectly square and plumb. Walls and floors may not be exactly straight, corners do not meet at precisely 90 degrees, and door and window jambs may be slightly askew. Anticipating these conditions and knowing how to adjust joints to fit will lead to success in finish carpentry.

The basic trim joints are the butt, mitered outside corner, and coped inside corner. A scarf joint joins two identical pieces of molding end to end. The ends of the molding are cut at parallel 45-degree angles and fitted together, one end overlapping the other. A scarf joint should be made over solid backing, such as a stud. Drill pilot holes through both pieces and secure the joint with finish nails.

*Installing trim around a room requires knowledge of several types of joints. Basic joinery includes the miter, scarf, and coped joints.*

## CUTTING A COPED JOINT

A coped joint allows two pieces of molding to meet at an inside corner. The method produces a tighter-fitting joint than an inside miter. To make the joint, butt one piece of trim to the corner and nail it in place.

Miter the second piece of trim across its face. (Don't cut it to length yet; do that after the joint is fitted.) You should see the mitered end when looking directly at the face of the molding (see the illustration on the opposite page). Clamp the molding face up on a rigid work surface. Then, using a coping saw held at 90 degrees to the face of the molding, carefully saw the outline of the molding profile—the line formed where the face of the molding meets the slanted miter cut. When the coping cut is finished, butt the coped piece of molding against the first. The joint should be tight and close-fitting. If not, reshape it slightly with small files or sandpaper. After you have fitted the joint, cut the molding to length.

## BACK-CUTTING BUTT JOINTS

To ensure a good fit, you can back-cut a butted or coped joint. Back-cutting means cutting at a slight angle so that the rear portion of the joint cannot interfere with a close fit at the front. A good example is when a piece of molding is butted into a corner. Typically, a small accumulation of wallboard compound exists in the corner, making it slightly concave rather than perfectly square. To compensate, the butted piece can be modified with a back cut. It is also possible to relieve the back edge of the joint slightly, using a chisel or file. Be careful not to take too much material or the back cut will be visible from above.

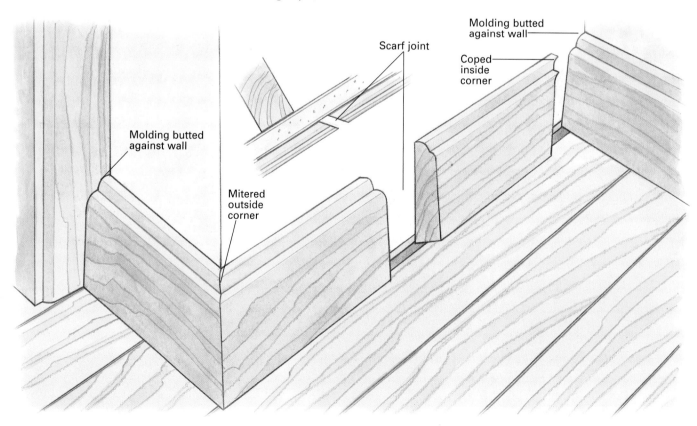

Scarf joint

Molding butted against wall

Coped inside corner

Molding butted against wall

Mitered outside corner

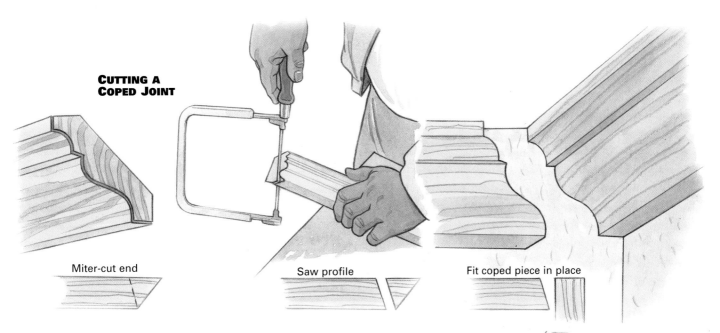

## CUTTING A COPED JOINT

Miter-cut end

Saw profile

Fit coped piece in place

*Cutting a coped joint for an inside corner requires butting the first piece of trim into the corner. The end of the second piece is mitered. Using the profile of the molding as a guide, cut out the miter square to the back surface of the trim, then butt the second piece to the first.*

## ADJUSTING MITERS

When miters don't meet perfectly, you can correct a small gap—⅛ inch or less—by recutting one side of the joint. Trim both pieces to fix a larger gap. Remember that trimming shortens your workpiece—too much could create problems on the other end.

Trim miters with a power miter saw. With care, the tool can shave small amounts with precision. Most power miter saws have positive stops at 90 and 45 degrees, making it difficult to adjust the blade angle by the small increment needed for readjusting miters. You can move the blade slightly, but when you tighten the locking screw, the blade slips back to the stop position. So, it's better to adjust the position of the workpiece against the miter box fence, as shown in the illustration at center right.

First, determine which part of the miter needs trimming, the heel or the toe. Set the workpiece against the miter box fence in a way that feels most comfortable—most people prefer to hold the workpiece with their left hand and operate the saw with their right. Set the blade angle. Slip a small shim—about the same thickness as the gap in the miter—between the fence and the trim. A piece of thin cardboard should work.

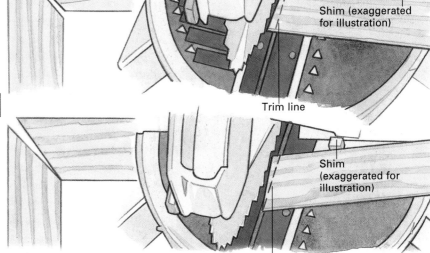

Shim (exaggerated for illustration)

Trim line

Shim (exaggerated for illustration)

Trim line

Hold the workpiece firmly against both the fence and the shim for cutting. When viewed from above, there will be a slight, triangular space behind the trim piece. If the short end, or heel, of the miter is toward the fence, then placing the shim close to the blade holds the millwork away from the fence slightly for trimming the heel. Placing the shim farther from the blade positions the millwork so the toe can be trimmed.

Position the piece carefully and hold it firmly. With your finger well away from the trigger, lower the blade and check the new angle you are about to cut. You must cut completely across the entire width of the millwork so that the new miter is straight. When you are satisfied with the position of the workpiece, raise the blade, start the motor, and recut the miter.

*Use small shims to position a miter-cut end so that it can be shaved a degree or two on the power miter box. Hold the workpiece firmly when cutting with a power miter box.*

# SAFETY

Face shield

Push sticks

Safety goggles

Ear plugs

Dust mask

afety equipment for finish carpentry is simple but essential. You need to properly protect yourself from dust and excessive noise with goggles or safety glasses, a dust mask or respirator, and ear plugs or sound-deadening muffs. Work gloves can protect your hands from abrasions and splinters, but don't wear them when operating power tools. Leather work shoes or boots will protect your feet better than running shoes.

Here are some tips that can help prevent workplace mishaps.

■ Use your common sense—that's the first rule of workplace safety. Don't work when you are tired, distracted, or angry. Make sure you have adequate lighting. Don't attempt heavy lifting or awkward tasks that can be done safely and more efficiently with a helper.

■ Tuck in loose-fitting clothing and tie back long hair. Remove rings, watch, and other jewelry when working with tools. Don't roll up the sleeves of a long-sleeve shirt—they may come undone at an inopportune moment. Wear them long and button the cuffs or switch to a short-sleeve shirt.

■ Keep the job site picked up and swept clean. Don't leave materials or cut-off waste on the floor—put it in a trash container. Store tools out of the way when not in use.

■ Use push sticks when operating a table saw. Avoid cutting short pieces.

■ Beware of kickback on a table saw. This occurs when a blade tooth catches a cut-off piece, trapped between the saw fence and the blade, and hurls it back toward the operator at high speed. Don't stand in line with the cutting line when sawing.

■ When using sharp cutting tools, such as chisels or utility knives, always cut away from you—never toward your body.

■ Clamp workpieces firmly to a solid support when working on them. Never saw a workpiece when supporting it with only your hand or leg.

■ Don't use corded power tools in wet or damp locations.

■ Be aware of the positions of your hands and feet before starting a power tool. When cutting curves with a saber saw, be careful that you don't wrap your fingers underneath the workpiece in the line of the cut.

■ Always use sharp tools. Dull tools may slip off the workpiece, mar it, or cause you to use undue force.

■ Make sure that adjustments on power tools are secured in the proper position before proceeding. Give locking knobs a final check before turning on the tool.

■ Unplug power tools before adjusting them or changing bits or blades.

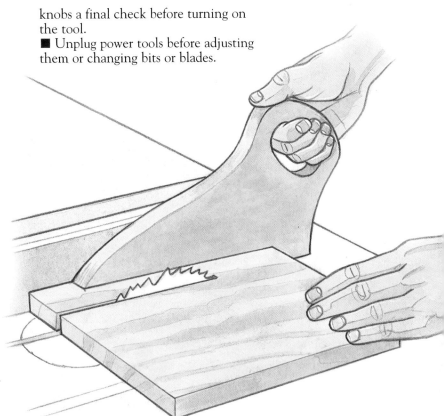

*A push stick keeps your fingers out of the dangerous area between the table-saw blade and fence, as shown above. Place your other hand well clear of the blade. Push the workpiece clear of the blade before letting go. When cutting crown molding on a power miter saw, support the molding solidly, as shown at the bottom. After making the cut, stop the saw before raising the blade.*

Block to support back of molding

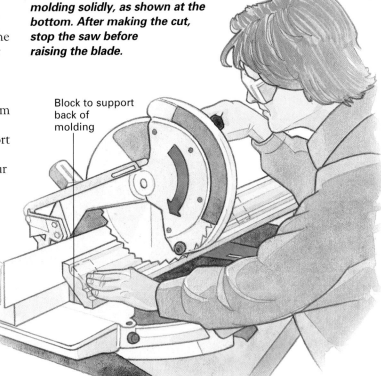

*Even an elaborate installation like this relies on basic finish carpentry techniques. Careful measuring and precise workmanship are essential for success.*

# BASIC INSTALLATIONS

Although finish carpentry is often associated with nailing up trim and decorative details, the skills of the finish carpenter are used for a variety of installation tasks. Adding wall paneling and wainscoting to walls, installing wood floors, and finishing stairs and railing systems are considered finish carpentry and require similar techniques and tools. As always, precise measuring, careful cutting, and patience are the keys to good results.

Some of these projects will proceed more efficiently if two people work together. Sheets of 4×8 wall paneling, for example, are not heavy, but they are awkward. A helping hand makes the job easier and safer. When installing flooring, have one person measure and install the flooring while another cuts the planks to length and positions them for nailing.

Be sure to store wood materials, such as paneling and flooring, in a dry place, preferably inside where the materials can become acclimated to the temperature and humidity where they'll be installed.

# WALL PANELING

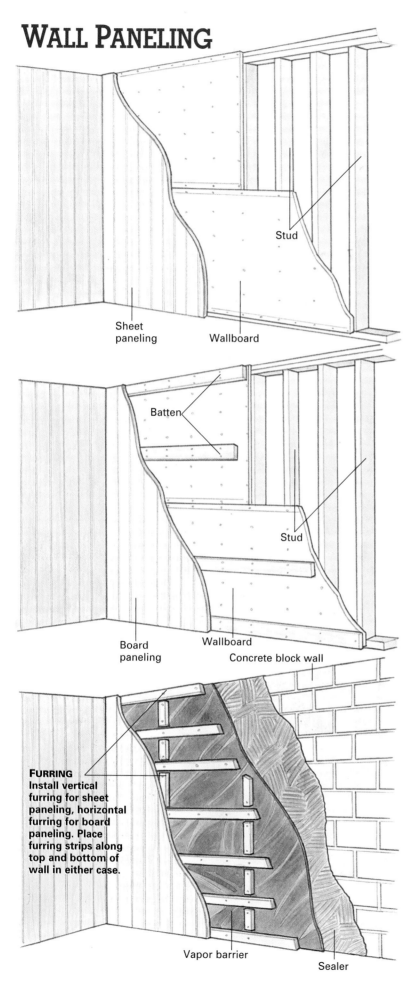

Stud

Sheet paneling

Wallboard

Batten

Stud

Board paneling

Wallboard

Concrete block wall

**FURRING**
Install vertical furring for sheet paneling, horizontal furring for board paneling. Place furring strips along top and bottom of wall in either case.

Vapor barrier

Sealer

There are two basic types of wall paneling: 4×8-foot sheet paneling and tongue-and-groove board paneling. Sheet paneling is plywood or hardboard covered with wood veneer, vinyl, or paper to look like vertical tongue-and-groove boards, wallpaper, tile, or other finish surfaces. Tongue-and-groove boards are solid wood, typically pine, cedar, or oak. The boards are nailed individually to the wall. Both types require proper preparation of the wall.

## INSTALLING SHEET PANELING

Sheet paneling goes up quickly. The time-consuming part of the job is preparing the walls to receive the paneling. Most building codes require fire-retardant wallboard behind paneling on a stud wall. The paneling is cut to length and installed over the studs, with the tops and bottoms of the panels nailed to the top and bottom plates, and nails driven every 8 inches along each stud. Each vertical joint between panels must fall directly over a stud so the edges can be securely nailed. Use color-matched panel nails that are long enough to go through the wallboard and penetrate at least ¾ inch into the studs.

Concrete or cement block walls must be furred out with strips of wood so that the panels can be securely nailed. First, seal the wall with concrete sealer or paint it with concrete paint that is rated as a moisture barrier. In a basement, install a barrier of 4-millimeter-thick plastic film as added protection against moisture. Install 1×3 wood battens along the top and bottom edges of the wall, spaced every 16 inches vertically across the face of the wall. Secure the battens with concrete nails.

Fasten the paneling with panel nails or panel adhesive—a specially formulated glue that comes in caulking-gun tubes. Follow the manufacturer's instructions when using the panel adhesive.

When installing paneling, start at a corner. The first panel must be installed plumb. If walls are not plumb, you'll need to scribe the paneling to fit the corner. Cut a panel to length and butt an edge to the corner, using a level to make sure the sheet is plumb. Use a compass or a scribing tool (shown on the opposite page) to trace the outline of the wall on the panel. Note that the opposite edge of the panel must fall at the middle of a stud or vertical batten for fastening. Preserve the factory edge opposite the

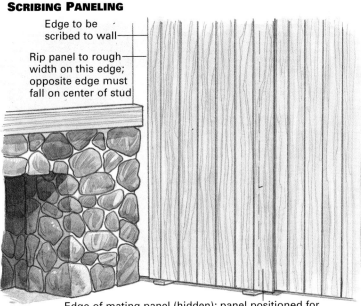

**SCRIBING PANELING**

Edge to be scribed to wall

Rip panel to rough width on this edge; opposite edge must fall on center of stud

Edge of mating panel (hidden); panel positioned for measuring corner panel, but not nailed in place yet

Hold compass level as you trace outline of irregular wall onto paneling

scribed edge so that the subsequent panel butts up to it cleanly. If you scribe the panel, then trim it to width on the opposite edge, the trim cut will probably not be perfect or the pattern on the face of the paneling will be interrupted awkwardly. It's better to cut off the excess on the scribed edge. If this means trimming a foot or so from the panel, rough cut it to width first, leaving 2 or 3 inches for scribing. Then plan the width of your scribe cut so that the opposite edge of the panel lands directly on a stud or vertical batten, as shown above. For a finished look, cover inside and outside corners with corner trim.

When ripping paneling, most power tools, such as a saber saw or circular saw, will splinter the top face. Use a plywood-cutting blade to minimize splintering. When possible, mark your cutting line on the back.

## INSTALLING BOARD PANELING

Tongue-and-groove board paneling goes up with the same general procedures as described for sheet paneling. Boards, however, require horizontal battens as a nailing surface, rather than studs or vertical battens. If your stud wall is open, you can let the battens into the framing before hanging the wallboard (illustrated on page 49). Put horizontal 1×3 battens 32 and 64 inches from the floor. The top and bottom of the paneling will be nailed to the top and bottom plates of the stud wall, and the middle portion to the battens.

Use a chalk line to mark cut lines along the studs as far apart as the width of the battens. Set the blade of a circular saw to cut the same depth as the thickness of the battens. Carefully cut each stud at the top and bottom

of the lines, then make several parallel cuts inside the lines to relieve the waste. Remove the waste with a chisel—the work goes rapidly. Install the battens—they should sit flush with the outside surface of the studs. Nail the battens in place with 8d common nails. Cover the wall with wallboard. If the wall is already enclosed with wallboard, install four horizontal runs of 1×3 battens at the top and bottom of the wall, and at 32 and 64 inches from the floor.

The first paneling board must be installed plumb; scribe it if necessary. Face-nail the first board, tongue edge out, to the battens. Subsequent boards are blind-nailed at a 45-degree angle just above the tongues. Use a level to check every third board to ensure they remain plumb. The last board may need to be scribed and ripped to fit. To do that, measure the distance from the wall to the inside of the V—the spot just above the tongue—of the next-to-last board. Measure at several places. Mark the longest distance at the top of the last board, but make this measurement from the groove side. Butt the last board to the wall, keeping it plumb. Set your compass or scribe to the distance between the mark at the top of the board and the wall. Scribe the length of the board. To install this last board, you may have to chisel away the rear portion of the groove.

PRO ADVICE: JAMB EXTENSIONS

Installing paneling, especially if battens are added over the wallboard, increases the wall's thickness, a factor that must be taken into account at windows and doors. You may need to add jamb extensions so that edges of jambs end up flush with the finish wall surfaces. Make jamb extensions by ripping ¾-thick (1×) material to the proper width to make up the difference. Nail the extensions carefully, predrilling each nail location.

# WAINSCOTING

Wainscoting is wood paneling that extends partway up a wall. The height is usually 36 to 42 inches from the floor, although wainscoting can be any height. Wainscoting provides rich detail and traditionally is used in living rooms, dining rooms, libraries, and dens. It is made of plywood, plywood paneling, or tongue-and-groove wood boards. The top of the wainscoting is covered with decorative molding—a cap rail.

## WAINSCOTING STYLES

The two most popular wainscoting methods are tongue-and-groove and frame-and-panel. Tongue-and-groove wainscoting comes as individual boards or grooved plywood panels that simulate the look of tongue-and-groove boards. Wainscoting boards typically are ¼ to ½ inch thick and are often sold cut to length and prepackaged at home improvement centers. The wood may be pine, oak, or mahogany. Plywood panels are usually ⅜ inch thick and come in a variety of styles, such as cedar and knotty pine. Some home improvement centers sell panels precut at 36 inches high.

Frame-and-panel wainscoting is made of plywood sheets with a framework of boards installed over the sheets to divide it into a pattern of rectangles. This framework consists of horizontal top and bottom rails with vertical stiles or mullions placed at regular intervals. The stiles are spaced to cover vertical seams between pieces of plywood. To add texture, miter and install decorative molding around the inside of the rectangles.

This basic design can be embellished. For instance, the inside edges of the stiles and rails can be detailed with a router after installation, or the molding can be held away from the edges of the stiles and rails to create a frame within a frame. Before beginning, sketch your ideas completely on a piece of paper so you'll have a clear idea of how to proceed. Once the panels and framework are nailed up, complete the installation with a cap rail and baseboard.

An elaborate version of frame-and-panel wainscoting features panels of solid wood with tapered edges that fit into dadoes cut in the edges of the stiles and rails. Only a skilled woodworker with the proper tools for creating the tapered edges of the panels should attempt this type of construction.

Wainscoting requires a solid backing of horizontal battens for nailing the tops and bottoms of boards and panels. If the wall is open, let the battens in to the wall framing, using the techniques described for wall paneling on page 47, or install blocking between the studs. This prevents the

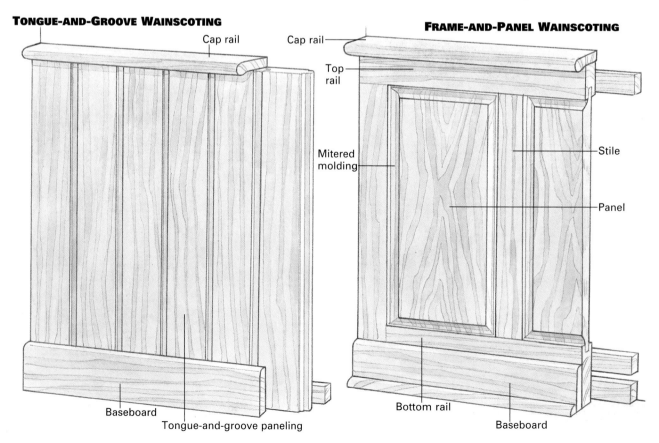

**TONGUE-AND-GROOVE WAINSCOTING**

Cap rail

Baseboard

Tongue-and-groove paneling

**FRAME-AND-PANEL WAINSCOTING**

Cap rail

Top rail

Mitered molding

Stile

Panel

Bottom rail

Baseboard

wainscoting from being too thick. Building codes require that the framing must then be covered with fire-retardant wallboard before the wainscoting is installed.

If the wall is already covered with wallboard, apply the battens over the wallboard, nailing them to the studs with 8d common or box nails, or with 2½-inch-long wallboard screws. The wainscoting attaches to the battens.

## PLANNING FOR WINDOW AND DOOR CASINGS

The hardest part of installing wainscoting is deciding what to do where the wainscoting meets window and door casings. Typically, wainscoting—with cap rail and baseboards—is thicker than casings, so it's best to figure a method of joining all components before the project begins. If the wainscoting is installed on battens that are let into the framing, the problem is simplified. In that case, the wainscot paneling butts directly against door casings, the baseboard is finished with a return detail at the edge of the casings (see page 65), and the cap rail is notched to fit around the casing with a finishing detail called a horn (see illustration on page 50).

At existing windows, start by removing the apron. Next, calculate what the stool detail will look like if the wainscot panels are nailed up and the apron reinstalled on top of the wainscoting. If there is at least ¾ inch between the front of the apron and the front edge of the stool (and the detail will not look awkward), then proceed. Rather than notch the paneling around the horn of the stool, notch the horn and slip the wainscoting behind it. The back end of the notch should be in line with the outside edge of the casings, so that when the paneling is installed, it butts tightly against both. Reinstall the apron. Measure and mark the cap rail to create a short horn that wraps around the front of the window casing for a finishing detail.

If you decide the stool is too narrow for the method described above, mark the edge of the window casings on the wall, then remove the stool and casings. You'll need to buy a wider stool or cut an extension for the existing stool. Nail up the wainscot paneling, stopping at the marks on the wall and cutting the paneling to fit under the window opening. Reinstall the new stool, the apron, and the casings. Measure and mark the cap rail to create a short horn that fits over the window casing.

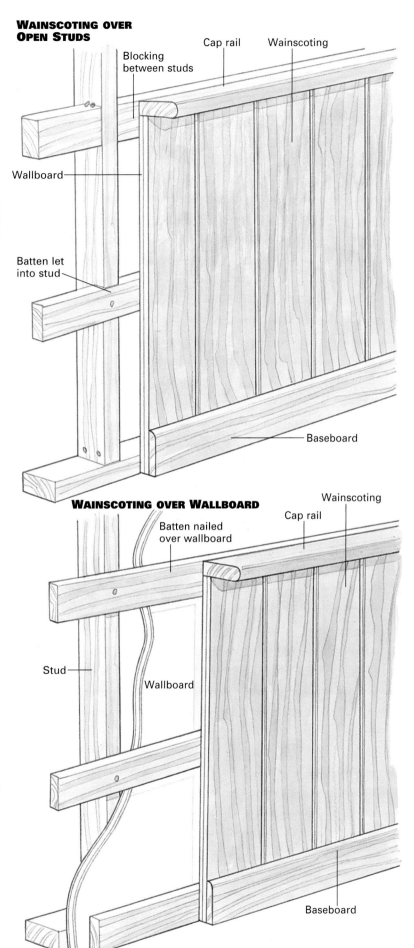

**WAINSCOTING OVER OPEN STUDS**

Blocking between studs · Cap rail · Wainscoting · Wallboard · Batten let into stud · Baseboard

**WAINSCOTING OVER WALLBOARD**

Batten nailed over wallboard · Wainscoting · Cap rail · Stud · Wallboard · Baseboard

# WAINSCOTING
*continued*

**TRIM FOR WAINSCOTING**

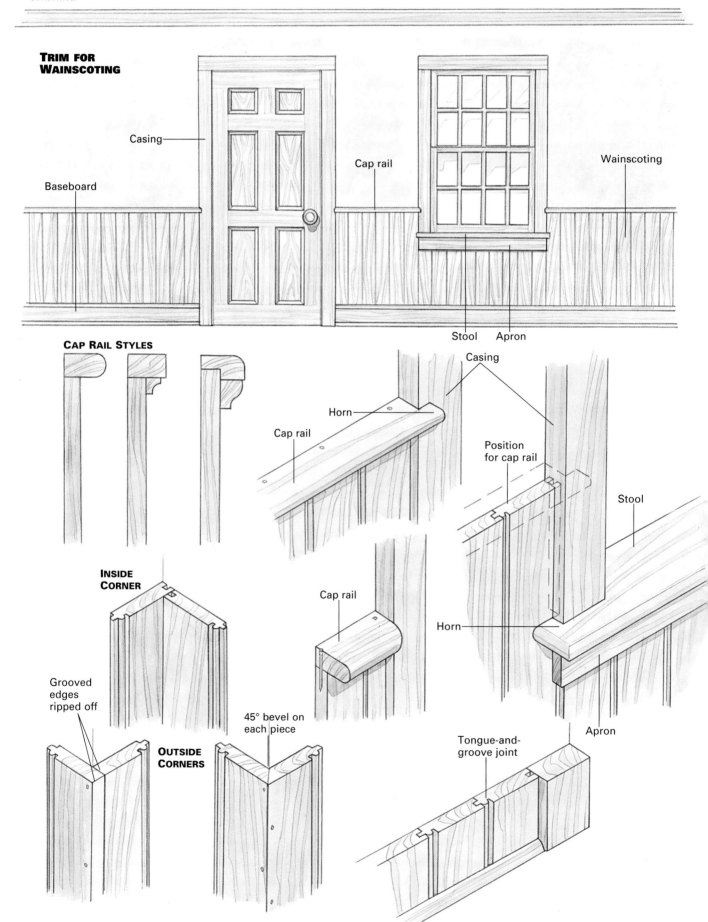

Casing

Baseboard

Cap rail

Wainscoting

Stool   Apron

**CAP RAIL STYLES**

Casing

Horn

Cap rail

Cap rail

Position for cap rail

Stool

**INSIDE CORNER**

Grooved edges ripped off

**OUTSIDE CORNERS**

45° bevel on each piece

Cap rail

Horn

Tongue-and-groove joint

Apron

If you install frame-and-panel wainscoting or wainscoting on battens attached to the outside of the wall, the wainscoting profile will be thick—2 inches or more. If so, cut and install jamb extensions and a new window stool. The extensions must be wide enough so that the door casings will sit on top of them, and they must be thick enough so that the wainscot paneling butts to them cleanly. Begin by removing all door and window trim, then cut the extensions from solid wood. Nail extensions flush to the inside of the existing jambs or hold them back ¼ to ⅜ of an inch to create a detail. Reinstall the casings on top of the extensions, then install paneling, baseboards, and cap rails as described before.

At electrical outlets and phone jacks, install box extensions. Determine the thickness of your wainscoting and buy the correct size extensions. Code-approved extensions that attach easily to boxes are available at hardware stores and home improvement centers.

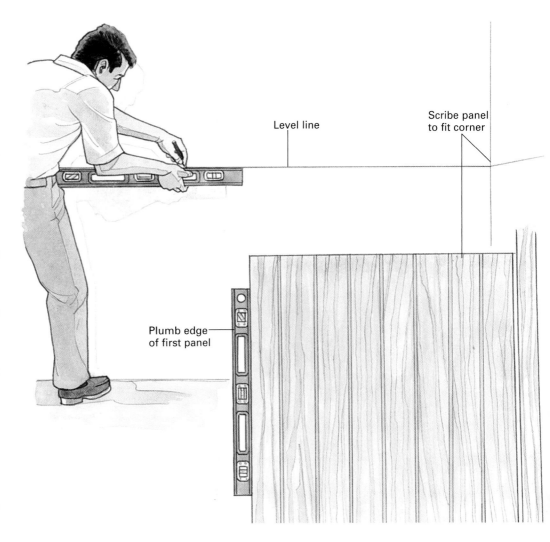

Level line

Scribe panel to fit corner

Plumb edge of first panel

## INSTALLING WAINSCOT PANELING

First, snap a level chalk line to indicate the height of the paneling. If you are nailing up battens over the wallboard, use a stud finder to locate all studs. Use the chalk line as a guide for installing the top batten, and drive two 8d common nails or 2½-inch-long wallboard screws at each stud location. Fasten the bottom batten directly into the bottom plate. Install the paneling, beginning at a corner. If necessary, scribe the first board or the edge of the plywood panel so that it is plumb and fits into the corner snugly. Install the remainder of the paneling, checking every third board with a level to make sure edges stay plumb. At electrical outlets, measure accurately and transfer the measurements

carefully. Make cutouts with a saber saw. Attach base and cap moldings, using the methods described for base moldings (pages 68–71) and chair rail (pages 72–73).

## INSTALLING FRAME-AND-PANEL WAINSCOTING

For frame-and-panel installations, first install battens, if necessary, using the method described for paneling, above. Then nail up the plywood panels, scribing them to the corners for a snug fit. Nail or screw the panels every 8 inches along the edges, using 8d common nails or 2½-inch-long wallboard screws. To install the frame, preassemble all the stiles and rails. First, lay out the pieces, making sure stiles will cover any seams between adjacent sheets of plywood. Mark the locations of the stiles on the upper and lower rails. Attach the stiles to the rails using glue and dowels or biscuits (pages 36–37). Clamp the assembly until it's dry, then install it as a unit. Attach base and cap moldings, using the methods described for base moldings (pages 68–71) and chair rail (pages 72–73).

# WOOD FLOORS

Installing flooring requires proper preparation of the subfloor, removing base shoe moldings, and repetitive tasks such as measuring, cutting, and fitting the individual pieces of flooring. Once you are familiar with the basics of installation, the work proceeds smoothly. This is a good job for two people—one to measure and install, the other to cut the pieces and lay them in place.

**SOLID WOOD STRIP OR PLANK FLOORING:** Strips are about 2½ inches wide; planks are 3 to 8 inches wide. Both are about ¾ inch thick, have tongue-and-groove edges, and are made from solid hardwoods, such as oak, maple, cherry, and walnut. More exotic species are available by special order from a flooring dealer or home improvement center. Solid flooring comes unfinished or prefinished. Because it is wood, the dimensions of the flooring may change slightly with the seasons. Store solid wood flooring inside at the job site for three or four days before installation to stabilize it.

*Wood and laminated floor coverings are relatively easy to install.*

Professional installers usually prefer unfinished flooring. Once the flooring is installed, the floor pros fill imperfections and seams with a paste filler, then sand the surface smooth with a flooring sander. The floor is then sealed and finished. Prefinished flooring eliminates the need for sanding and finishing, which makes it a better choice for do-it-yourself installation.

**COMPOSITE WOOD FLOORING:** This flooring features a prefinished hardwood veneer bonded to a ⅜-inch-thick layer of plywood or hardboard. The veneer typically is oak or maple, often stained. This type of flooring cannot be resanded.

Due to its laminated construction, it remains stable during changes in temperature and humidity. It is lightweight, cuts easily, and is a good material for do-it-yourself installations.

Composite flooring comes as strips, planks, or parquet squares that are glued to the subfloor with mastic—nailing is not necessary. Once the flooring installation is complete, the entire surface is rolled with a heavy flooring roller to ensure a good bond.

**PLASTIC LAMINATE FLOORING:** It looks like wood, but this flooring is plastic. It also shares many of the same characteristics and basic installation requirements as wood. It's durable, maintenance-free, and simple to install. The strips or planks are topped with a layer of plastic that looks like various types of wood, and the cost is comparable to composite wood flooring. Laminate flooring is installed as a floating floor—the material is not glued or fastened directly to the subfloor. Instead, the flooring pieces are laid over a thin polyethylene foam pad and glued to each other with white glue. The completed floor can withstand heavy foot traffic.

## PREPARING THE SUBFLOOR

Solid wood flooring must be nailed to a solid wood or plywood subfloor at least ¾ inch thick. The flooring can be nailed over vinyl flooring if the vinyl is applied directly to a solid wood or plywood subfloor. Otherwise, old floor coverings should be removed before installing solid wood flooring.

Composite flooring can be glued to any material that is tightly bonded to the subfloor, level, and free of defects such as cracks or warps. Glue composite flooring directly to concrete, vinyl, wood, or plywood. Smooth tile with a latex floor leveling compound before installing composite flooring.

Plastic laminate installs over virtually any surface, including tile. Because it is not fastened with glue or nails, a floating floor can be installed over concrete, brick, tile, vinyl, and wood that is in good condition and free of defects.

Prepare for installation by removing all base shoe molding. If possible, preserve the pieces of base shoe and number them for easier reinstallation. If there is no base shoe, you'll need to remove the baseboard molding. During installation, leave a ½-inch gap between the flooring and the walls to allow for expansion. The base shoe or baseboard will cover this gap.

Saw off the bottoms of all door casings and door stops—but not the door jambs. This allows you to slip the flooring under the casings and stop for a neat appearance. In a bathroom, you'll need to remove the toilet—

stuff a rag in the drain opening to prevent sewer gas from entering the room. In a kitchen, be aware of what the change in floor level will mean for built-in appliances, such as a dishwasher. Measure carefully to determine if you have enough room under countertops to reposition the appliances once the new flooring is installed. If your appliance has adjustable legs, you may be able to shorten them to accommodate the level of the new flooring. If not, you can adjust the countertop height with shims—a big job. Do not install flooring up to the front of an appliance, trapping it in the opening. It may be easier to buy a new dishwasher that fits the space.

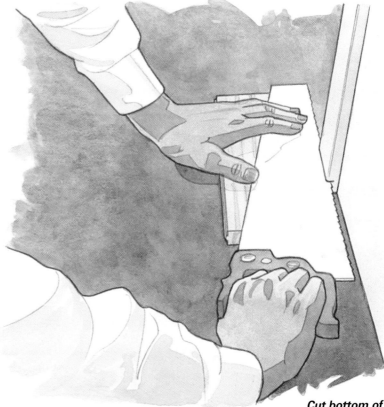

Cut bottom of door casings and stops to clear new flooring. A scrap piece of flooring under the saw will ensure a level cut at the right height.

## PLANNING THE LAYOUT

If you are installing flooring in only one room, begin at one wall and work all the way across the room. If you will install flooring in two or more adjacent rooms, plan which direction the strips will run. This is especially important for long, narrow spaces, such as hallways, where boards should run lengthwise. If you change directions of the flooring, do it at a doorway, planning the layout so that the last piece of flooring of one room runs across the doorway with an exposed tongue. In the adjacent room, butt the grooved ends of flooring to this tongue.

When installing strip or plank flooring, the width of the last piece isn't important—a narrow piece won't disrupt the pattern. For wood parquet squares, work from the center out. First, dry-lay the squares across the room to determine a starting point. Adjust the layout so that the squares at the edges will be equal and not too narrow. Then snap perpendicular lines from wall to wall, dividing the room into equal quadrants and establishing the central starting point.

## INSTALLING SOLID WOOD FLOORING

A flooring nailer speeds this job. This hand-held tool holds specially designed flooring nails and is designed to blind-nail the flooring at a 45-degree angle just above the tongue. The tool is operated by striking a plunger with a mallet. Rent a flooring nailer at any rental shop that carries tools. Ask the dealer to show you how to use the tool. Because of the design of the tool, it is not possible to use it when nailing the starter course or the last few rows of flooring. Face-nail these boards

without using the flooring nailer.

Solid-wood flooring installation begins with a starter course laid parallel to one wall. Snap a chalk line ½ inch away from the wall. Lay out the first row, tongue side out, keeping the ends ½ inch from the end walls. Make sure any end seams are butted tightly. Predrill straight down into each board and fasten the boards to the subfloor with 8d finish nails driven every 16 inches and 2 inches from each end. Set the nailheads below the surface of the boards. Because the flooring nailer generates a lot of force, it's a good idea to face-nail a second row of flooring. With two courses of flooring nailed down this way, the force of the nailer won't jar the starter row out of alignment.

Work your way across the floor, staggering end butt joints at least 6 inches apart. Use the mallet to tap boards into position before nailing. To keep the work progressing efficiently, measure and precut several rows of flooring and arrange the pieces loosely on the floor, then install those rows. Having two people—one to measure and nail, one to cut and lay out the loose pieces of flooring—speeds the process.

When you get near the opposite wall, you won't have enough room to swing the mallet for the flooring nailer. You'll need to switch to face nailing again to finish the work. Place a scrap block of wood against the wall and use a pry bar to force the last row tightly into place before nailing.

# WOOD FLOORS
*continued*

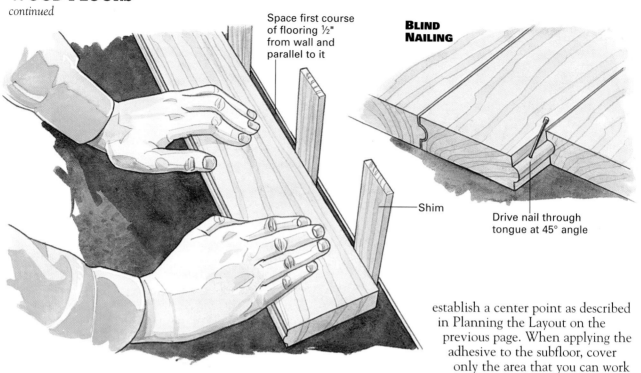

Space first course of flooring ½" from wall and parallel to it

Shim

Drive nail through tongue at 45° angle

## INSTALLING GLUE-DOWN FLOORING

Composite strip and parquet flooring is installed using an adhesive on a dry, level subfloor. Trowel on the adhesive according to the manufacturer's instructions. For composite strips, begin by snapping a straight chalk layout line parallel to one wall. For parquets,

establish a center point as described in Planning the Layout on the previous page. When applying the adhesive to the subfloor, cover only the area that you can work on during the manufacturer's recommended drying time. Use a mallet and a scrap of flooring as a block to gently tap pieces of flooring into alignment and to tighten all joints. To ensure a good bond between the flooring and the subfloor, go over finished sections of flooring with a flooring roller—a heavy, hand-operated tool available at rental stores. Roll the floor within two hours of installation.

*A flooring nailer speeds installation of solid-wood flooring. The tool forces the tongue-and-groove joint together as it drives a nail at the correct angle.*

*Place a scrap piece of flooring over the tongue of a strip as you drive it into place. This protects the tongue from damage, and ensures a tight joint.*

## PRO ADVICE: WORKING WITH WARPED WOOD

Warped flooring boards are difficult to install. Since flooring is expensive, you won't want to throw them away. If possible, cut them into smaller, more manageable lengths, discarding only the worst sections. Or, buy a hardwood flooring bar. This clawlike bar can be used to grip the edge of the starter row. From there, put a bar clamp with one jaw on the warped board and the other on the upturned end of the flooring bar. To prevent damage to the tongue of the warped board, place a piece of scrap flooring between the jaw of the clamp and the board. Use the clamp to force the warped board into position for nailing.

*Lever the last course of tongue-and-groove flooring into place to make a tight joint. Face-nail the board.*

## MAKING CUTOUTS WITH TEMPLATES

Install flooring around corners or other irregular areas by first test-fitting a template made of cardboard. Cut the template the same width as your flooring, then transfer measurements for your cutout to the template and cut it with a utility knife. Test-fit the template. If you're satisfied, trace the outline of the template onto a piece of flooring for a final cut.

## INSTALLING A FLOATING FLOOR

Floating floor installations, such as those required for plastic laminate flooring, include many of the same layout procedures as wood flooring. The difference is that a floating floor is not fastened to the subfloor. Instead, the edges of the flooring are glued to each other and the resulting membrane sits on top of a thin foam cushion. A floating floor can be installed over virtually any kind of existing flooring—wood, tile, vinyl—making it ideal for retrofits.

Follow the manufacturer's instructions for your flooring. Generally, you begin installation along one wall, leaving a ½-inch gap between the flooring and the wall. Be sure to glue end joints well, and wipe up excess glue from the surface of the boards immediately with a damp rag. As you work, keep your body weight off the installed sections of flooring for at least one hour, giving the glue time to dry thoroughly.

*Make a template to cut pieces for around obstructions. Glue the pieces in place after testing them for fit.*

*Apply glue to the edges and ends of laminated flooring to form a strong bond with all the parts of the floor.*

# STAIRS AND RAILINGS

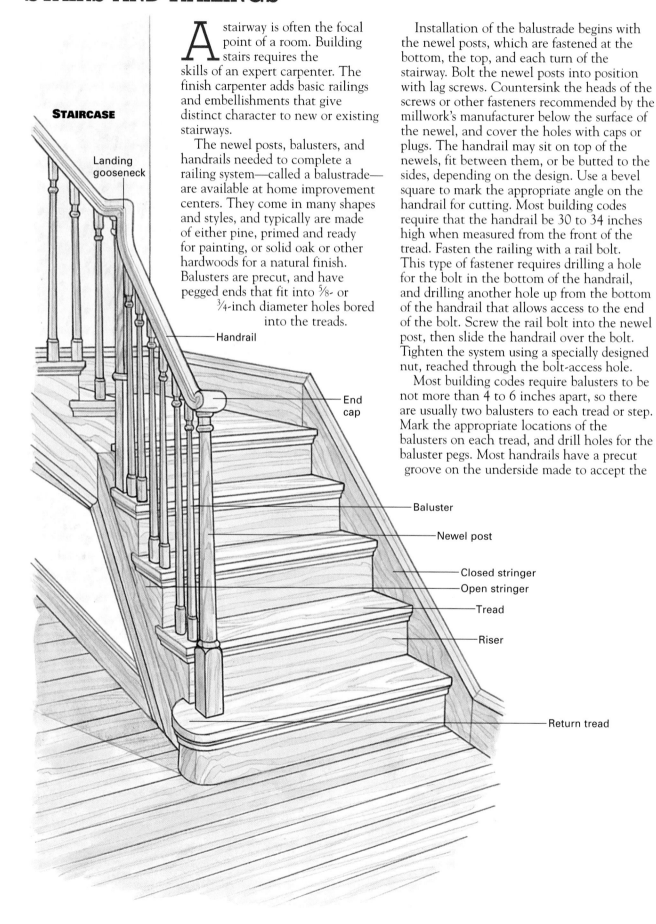

**STAIRCASE**

Landing gooseneck

Handrail

End cap

Baluster

Newel post

Closed stringer

Open stringer

Tread

Riser

Return tread

A stairway is often the focal point of a room. Building stairs requires the skills of an expert carpenter. The finish carpenter adds basic railings and embellishments that give distinct character to new or existing stairways.

The newel posts, balusters, and handrails needed to complete a railing system—called a balustrade—are available at home improvement centers. They come in many shapes and styles, and typically are made of either pine, primed and ready for painting, or solid oak or other hardwoods for a natural finish. Balusters are precut, and have pegged ends that fit into $\frac{5}{8}$- or $\frac{3}{4}$-inch diameter holes bored into the treads.

Installation of the balustrade begins with the newel posts, which are fastened at the bottom, the top, and each turn of the stairway. Bolt the newel posts into position with lag screws. Countersink the heads of the screws or other fasteners recommended by the millwork's manufacturer below the surface of the newel, and cover the holes with caps or plugs. The handrail may sit on top of the newels, fit between them, or be butted to the sides, depending on the design. Use a bevel square to mark the appropriate angle on the handrail for cutting. Most building codes require that the handrail be 30 to 34 inches high when measured from the front of the tread. Fasten the railing with a rail bolt. This type of fastener requires drilling a hole for the bolt in the bottom of the handrail, and drilling another hole up from the bottom of the handrail that allows access to the end of the bolt. Screw the rail bolt into the newel post, then slide the handrail over the bolt. Tighten the system using a specially designed nut, reached through the bolt-access hole.

Most building codes require balusters to be not more than 4 to 6 inches apart, so there are usually two balusters to each tread or step. Mark the appropriate locations of the balusters on each tread, and drill holes for the baluster pegs. Most handrails have a precut groove on the underside made to accept the tops of the balusters. Mark the vertical position of the balusters on the handrail and cut them to length. Predrill the balusters, then nail or screw them to the underside of the handrail.

The treads usually extend over the risers and the stringers. Add decorative moldings (a cove molding works well) beneath the edge and end of the tread for a finished appearance. Miter the molding at the corners, and finish the exposed end with a return miter or a beveled cut.

Add flair with a decorative bracket or scroll under the side of each tread. Buy premade decorative brackets and scrolls at home improvement centers, and fix them to the stringer with epoxy cement. Decorative brackets and scrolls are made of solid wood and can be stained or painted to match your finish scheme.

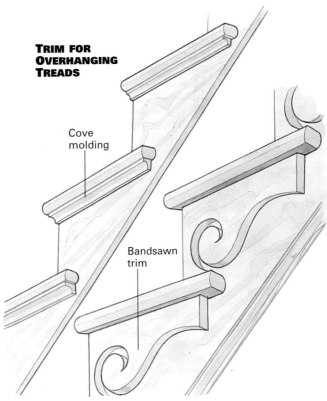

**TRIM FOR OVERHANGING TREADS**

Cove molding

Bandsawn trim

Return

Edging

*Hide the end grain of treads on an open riser with edging. Miter-cut the end of a piece of stock, then handsaw off a short block for a return. Glue the return into place.*

## SILENCING SQUEAKY STAIRS

Most staircase squeaks are caused by treads rubbing against stringers or risers. The problem occurs because wood shrinks over time, loosening parts and creating small gaps. When someone walks on the stairs, the loose parts rub against each other, causing squeaks. To silence those squeaks, you need to refasten the stair parts to each other, fixing them in position.

If you can get to the underside of the staircase, the best solution is to add blocks or braces. Cut hardwood blocks to fit at the angle formed by the riser and the tread. Glue and screw the blocks to both the riser and tread. You also can use metal angle brackets, available at hardware stores and home improvement centers. Predrill holes for screws.

If you can't get to the underside of the staircase, drive screws down through the tread into the top of the riser. Use screws that will penetrate 1½ inches into the center of the riser. Use a counterbore to drill pilot holes for the screws, and fill the counterbore holes with plugs cut from matching wood. Another solution is to coat the ends of small, thin wood shims with glue, then drive the wedges into the seam at the back of the tread where it meets the riser. Cut off the shim with a utility knife, and cover the seam with quarter-round or base shoe molding.

# WORKING WITH TRIMS AND MOLDINGS

Trim and molding serve three basic functions. They hide imperfections and gaps, such as the seam between wall finishes and door jambs. They perform utilitarian functions, such as picture rails used to hang artwork and chair rails used to prevent damage to walls. Trim and molding also contribute to architectural style and provide decorative effects. Sometimes, highly detailed molding adds as much character to a room as any furniture or accessory.

Hanging trims and moldings is a primary responsibility of the finish carpenter. Patience and attention to detail will ensure that the job enhances—not detracts from—a room's appearance. Even simple schemes and plain moldings benefit from skilled workmanship.

Millwork requires special handling. The pieces are often long, sometimes delicate, and easily damaged. Take care when moving molding around the job site. Be aware of where both ends are, and always support moldings adequately so they don't break. When cutting or shaping moldings, clamp them firmly to the work surface to prevent vibration. When cutting millwork in with a power miter box, make sure the outboard ends rest on a block or other support that is exactly the same height as the table of the tool.

Unless you use an air nailer, you should always predrill moldings before nailing to prevent splits and cracks, even toward the middle of a piece of paint-grade molding. Few things are more frustrating than installing a 10-foot-long section of molding only to have it crack on the very last nail. Predrilling prevents nails from curving once they enter the wood, too, keeping the fastener straight.

In some cases, you may have to correct flaws in the rough carpentry in order to get acceptable results with your finish work. Careful work and attention to detail at this stage are the keys to good results.

**With care and patience, you can do high-quality trim and molding work like this.**

# WINDOW TRIM

Trim is applied to window interiors in any of several basic styles. The most common type (shown below as Mitered Casing with Stool) features a lower window edge trimmed with a stool—a flat piece installed horizontally to form a small ledge, often called a windowsill. Casing runs around the other three sides of the window and is butted into the stool. At the upper corners, the casings are mitered. Below the stool a piece of trim called an apron covers the gap between the window frame and the wall covering. The apron is wide enough to provide visual balance among all the elements of the trim. Here are some other styles:

**PICTURE FRAME:** This style, with basic casing on all four sides, and four mitered corners, is usually used on windows on the upper portion of a wall. Despite its simple appearance, it is not an easy task to produce four, tight-fitting, interdependent miter joints. Trimming one miter to fit can affect the angle at which the others meet or the lengths of the pieces, pulling other joints out of alignment.

**BUTTED HEAD:** This casing has no miters and is one of the easiest styles to fit properly. In this example, the head casing simply runs past the side casings by ½ to 1 inch, and the side casings butt to the underside.

**CABINET HEAD:** This variation of the butted head features a small piece of trim that sits on top of the head casing. Typically, the uppermost piece of trim is cut slightly larger than the thickness and length of the head casing so that it projects past the front and sides of the head casing. Cabinet head variations can be quite elaborate and are limited only by the carpenter's imagination and sense of proportion (see page 65).

**CORNER BLOCKS:** This style comes from the Victorian age, when millwork was first machine-made and sold in mass quantities. Using corner blocks made it relatively easy for finish carpenters to quickly hang elaborate,

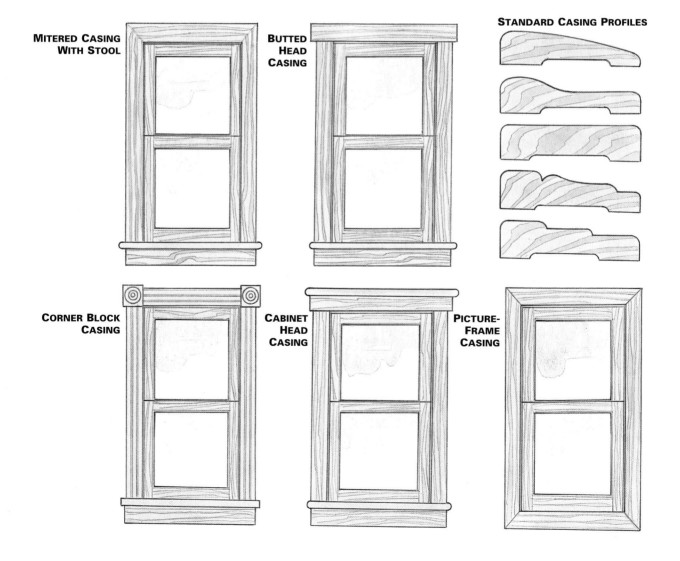

MITERED CASING WITH STOOL

BUTTED HEAD CASING

STANDARD CASING PROFILES

CORNER BLOCK CASING

CABINET HEAD CASING

PICTURE-FRAME CASING

**MAKING JAMBS
FLUSH WITH WALL**

Where the wall stands out from the jamb, add extensions to the jamb; if the difference is slight, take down the wall surface with coarse sandpaper, a rasp, or a shaping tool

Where the jamb stands out from the wall, plane or sand the jamb flush with the wall surface.

precarved moldings. The style calls for the corner blocks to be wider and thicker than the casings, making it a simple matter to butt the casings to the blocks. Corner blocks usually have round rosette carvings.

## ADJUSTING ROUGH CARPENTRY

Carefully inspect the entire window opening to make sure that the inside edge of the window jamb is flush with the surrounding wall surface. If not, you'll need to adjust the difference so that casings will lie flat when installed. It's not uncommon for the jamb and wall surface to be flush at one corner and out of alignment at another.

Most casings have a slight relief on their back face to accommodate minor differences in the wall finish and jambs. However, a difference of 1/8 inch or greater should be adjusted. If the jamb is below the wall by 1/8 to 1/4 inch, adjust the wall by shaving the wallboard with a serrated rasp. Only shave out a distance equal to the width of the casing. You want a smooth, flat surface that slopes slightly toward the jamb. Use a scrap piece of casing to test the work.

If the jamb is more than 1/4 inch below the wall surface, add a jamb extension. Make sure the extension is the same thickness as the jamb. The window will usually be out of alignment unevenly, so the extension will need to be thicker at one corner than the other. The best way to handle this situation is to cut the extension wider than necessary,

then glue it onto the jamb without nailing it. Use clamps or masking tape to hold the extension while the glue dries. Once dry, use a hand plane to shave the extension flush with the surrounding wall surfaces. Then drive two or three 4d finish nails through the extension into the jamb to hold it in position permanently. Another method is to hold the

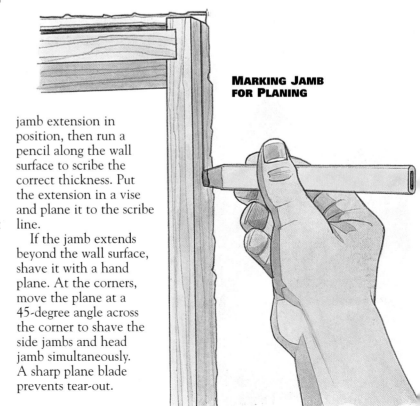

**MARKING JAMB
FOR PLANING**

jamb extension in position, then run a pencil along the wall surface to scribe the correct thickness. Put the extension in a vise and plane it to the scribe line.

If the jamb extends beyond the wall surface, shave it with a hand plane. At the corners, move the plane at a 45-degree angle across the corner to shave the side jambs and head jamb simultaneously. A sharp plane blade prevents tear-out.

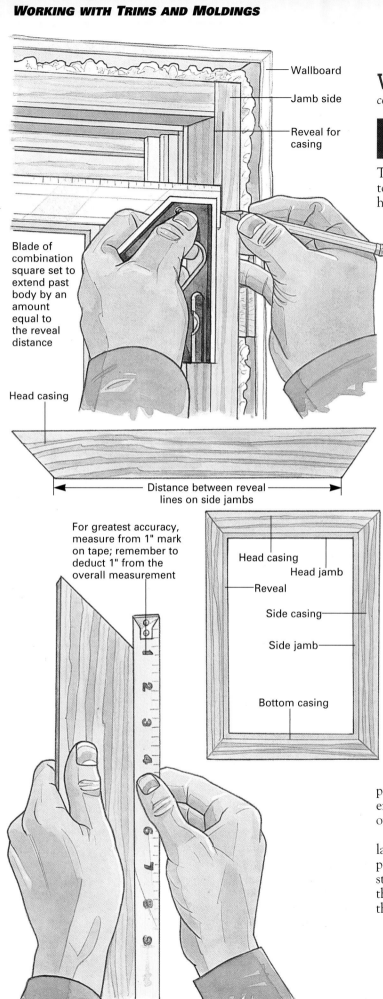

Wallboard

Jamb side

Reveal for casing

Blade of combination square set to extend past body by an amount equal to the reveal distance

Head casing

Distance between reveal lines on side jambs

For greatest accuracy, measure from 1" mark on tape; remember to deduct 1" from the overall measurement

Head casing

Head jamb

Reveal

Side casing

Side jamb

Bottom casing

# WINDOW TRIM

*continued*

## INSTALLING STOOLS AND APRONS

The first step in trimming out a window is to install the stool. Stool stock is available at home improvement centers. Seen in profile, stool stock is a thick molding with a beveled cutout on its underside. This bevel sits on top of the windowsill, which is slanted outward to shed water. The cutout fits snugly against the front edge of the sill to form a tight seal. The outside edge of the stool fits against the inside of the window sash, but not so tight that it interferes with window operation.

First, cut the stool to length. To find the length, determine the distance between the jambs, add the width of both side casings, the width of both reveals (the reveal is the distance between the inside of the jamb and the edge of the casing, typically ¼ inch), and 1 inch on either end for a finishing detail.

Mark the center of the window opening on the sill, then mark the center of the stool. Align the two marks. On the stool, mark the inside edges of both jambs, as shown in the illustration at top left on the opposite page.

Close the window, and measure the distance from the back of the stool to the window sash. Subtract $\frac{1}{16}$ inch for clearance, and set a compass to this distance for scribing. (If you measured 1 inch, set the scribing compass to $\frac{15}{16}$ inch.) Then scribe the ends of the stool for cutting, guiding the point of the compass along the wall surface. Scribing these cuts ensures a tight fit against the wall.

Use a square to extend the lines that indicate the inside edges of the jambs to intersect the scribed lines. Then, cut out the corners to form the stool horns.

The stool should now fit snugly into position—notched against the wall at both ends, with an inner edge that sits on top of the sill in front of the window sash.

To fasten the stool, apply a bead of acrylic latex caulk to the underside and place it in position. Predrill down through the top of the stool and the sill at a slight angle, aiming for the rough framing sill. Drive 12d finish nails through the stool, sill, and into the rough sill.

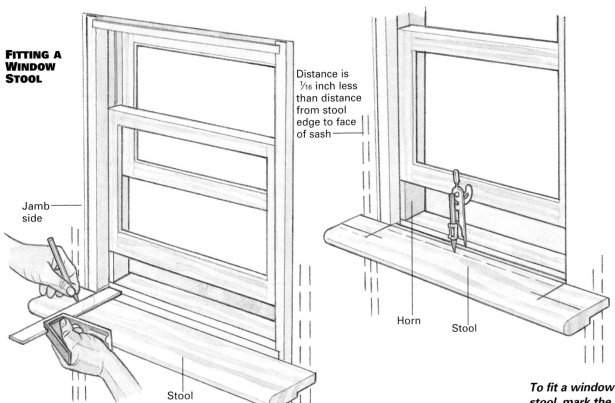

**FITTING A WINDOW STOOL**

Jamb side

Stool

Distance is 1/16 inch less than distance from stool edge to face of sash

Horn

Stool

*To fit a window stool, mark the distance between the jamb sides on the stool, using a combination square for accuracy. Scribe the outside edge of the stool to meet the sill, then scribe the horns to meet the casing sides. Test-fit the stool, and cut the horns to length.*

Cut the apron from the same stock as the casing. The length should equal the width of the installed side casings, measured from their outside edges. Install the apron with the thickest part of the molding against the stool, and bevel the ends at about 7 degrees. If your apron is made from a complex piece of molding, give the ends a return miter for a more finished appearance. Nail down through the stool into the top of the apron with 8d finish nails spaced every 12 inches.

## INSTALLING MITERED CASINGS

Establish a reference line on the edge of the window jambs for the reveal—the amount of the edge of the jamb that will be exposed after the casings are installed. A typical reveal is 1/4 inch wide. Mark the reveal by setting the blade of a combination square to 1/4 inch. Use the square to mark a consistent reveal all the way around the window jambs.

Begin the installation with the head casing. Measure between the side reveals to determine the length of the head casing. This distance is the length between the heels—or insides—of the miter cuts. You won't be able to hook the end of your measuring tape over the heel of the miter, so you'll have to hold the tape alongside the casing to measure. In

this position, it can be difficult to establish an accurate measurement from the end of the tape. For more accuracy, "pull an inch" by measuring to the 1-inch mark instead of the very end of the tape. Remember to subtract the extra inch from your overall measurement when establishing a line for cutting.

Install the head casing first. Align the heels with the reveal marks that indicate the side casings. Hang the head casing with a single 8d finish nail driven partway into the framing. Leave the nailhead above the surface for now; you might need to remove the head casing for trimming.

Miter the ends of the side casings, but leave them long. Position each casing upside down, with the toe of the miter against the stool. Be careful not to blunt the toe of the miter. Slide the casing against the head casing and mark where the toe of the head casing touches the side casing. Make a square cut at this mark. Using the reveal marks as guides, install the casings with 8d finish nails driven every 12 inches into the framing and 4d nails driven every 12 inches into the window jambs. Always predrill at the ends of the casings. If the miters need trimming or adjustments, use the techniques described in Trim Joinery on page 40.

# WINDOW TRIM
*continued*

## HANGING PICTURE-FRAME CASINGS

The picture-frame style has four miter joints. The first two joints are easy to make, but the third and fourth require some adjustments to get them just right. That's because small imperfections in the wall surfaces, the moldings, and the angle of the miter saw all add up and reveal themselves at those last miter joints. If you are fussy about good joinery and have a piece of molding to spare, try this technique.

First, mark reveals on the edges of all the jambs. Use the reveals to determine the length of side casings and head and bottom casings, as measured to the heel of the miters. Hang the head casing and two side casings as described in Installing Mitered Casings on the previous page. Miter the ends of your spare piece of molding, but cut this piece 1 inch short. Using the reveal marks as a guide, place the spare molding in position and slide it to one side. Check this miter for fit. If it's off, trim the miter of your spare piece to make a tight joint. When you are satisfied, slide the molding to the other miter and check this fit. Trim again if necessary.

When both bottom miters are tight, use your spare piece of molding to transfer the proper miter angles to your actual bottom casing, making sure to cut the actual casing to its proper length. Install the casings with 8d finish nails driven every 12 inches into the framing, and 4d nails driven every 12 inches into the

Head casing nailed in place

Mark bottom of side casing at top of head casing for straight cut

Top of side casing

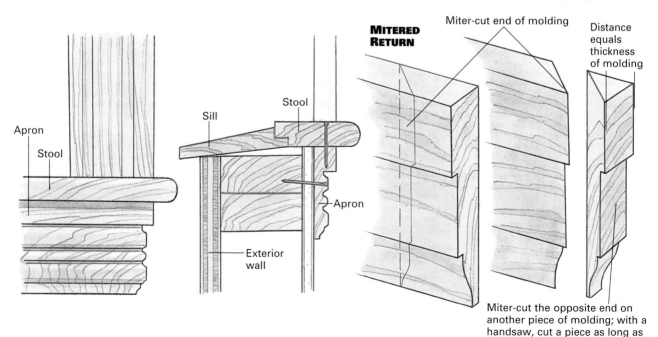

Apron

Stool

Sill

Stool

Apron

Exterior wall

**MITERED RETURN**

Miter-cut end of molding

Distance equals thickness of molding

Miter-cut the opposite end on another piece of molding; with a handsaw, cut a piece as long as the thickness of the molding; glue return in place

window jambs. Always predrill at the ends of the casings.

## INSTALLING BUTTED CASINGS

Mark the reveals on the edges of the jambs, using a combination square set to ¼ inch. Cut the side jambs to length, measuring between the stool and the reveal mark for the head jamb. Hang them temporarily in position with a single 8d finish nail driven only partway in. Leave the nailhead exposed in case you need to remove the casing to trim the ends. The bottom of the side casings should sit flush on the stool with no gaps. Cut the head casing to length—it should hang over the outside edges of the side casings by ¾ to 1 inch. Check the fit of the butt joints. If they do not meet perfectly, mark the difference on the end of the casing, making sure to indicate which corner is high and needs trimming. Trim the casing with your power miter box (see Trim Joinery, page 40). When the butt joints are tight, nail the casings in place with 8d finish nails driven every 12 inches into the framing, and 4d nails driven every 12 inches into the window jambs. Always predrill at the ends of the casings.

More elaborate head casing designs, such as the cabinet head casing at right, usually are made of several pieces of molding. However, the installation techniques are identical. Instead of nailing up the pieces individually, build the cabinet head as a single unit, then install it in one piece. This ensures that the butt joints between the head and side casings are tight.

## INSTALLING CORNER BLOCKS

When hanging casings to corner blocks, the blocks are installed first, with the inside lower corners just touching the intersection of the lines indicating the jamb reveals. To begin, use only a single 8d finish nail driven partway into each block. This allows you to turn the block slightly to make fine adjustments.

Install the head casing, trimming for a precise fit. When you're satisfied, secure the head casing and corner blocks. Trim the side casings to fit, and install them with 8d finish nails driven every 12 inches into the framing, and 4d nails driven every 12 inches into the window jambs.

**CABINET HEAD WINDOW CASING**

Cabinet head

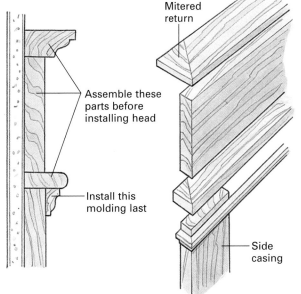

*A cabinet head butts against the tops of the casing sides. Assemble casing head before installing it. Finish the molding ends with mitered returns. The molding at the bottom of the head goes on last.*

Mitered return

Assemble these parts before installing head

Install this molding last

Side casing

# DOOR TRIM

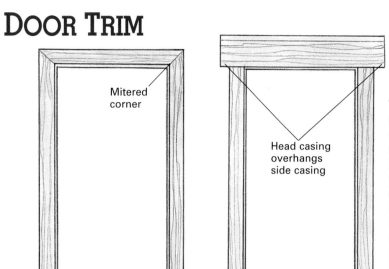

Mitered corner

Head casing overhangs side casing

Trimming out a door is generally pretty quick work because, unlike a window, there is no bottom piece. To produce neat, professional-looking results, carefully plan how the door casings will meet base moldings, wall paneling, and wainscoting. For more information see Baseboards, pages 68–71, and Wainscoting, pages 48–51. Here are some styles for door casings:

**PICTURE FRAME:** This style of casing is mitered at the upper corners. This is a relatively simple installation and one of the most common.

**BUTTED HEAD:** This casing has no miters and is one of the easiest styles to fit properly. The head casing simply runs past the side casings by ½ to 1 inch, and the side casings butt to the underside.

**CABINET HEAD:** In this variation on the butted head casing, a more elaborate cabinet head replaces the plain head casing.

**VICTORIAN:** Butt-joined casings with plinth blocks and corner blocks were first mass-produced in the Victorian Era. The blocks make it easy for finish carpenters to hang moldings quickly. The corner blocks are wider and thicker than the casings, and the plinths are wider and thicker than both the casings and the base molding. The baseboards and casings butt up to the blocks, providing some room for error.

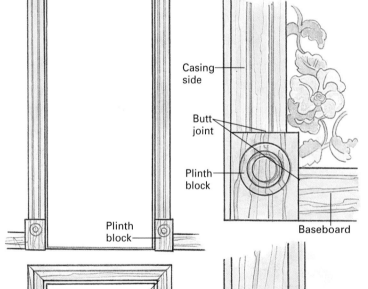

Corner block

Casing side

Butt joint

Plinth block

Plinth block

Baseboard

Mitered corner

Casing side

Mitered corner

Baseboard cap

Baseboard

Butt joint

## ADJUSTING ROUGH CARPENTRY

Use a plumb bob or a long straightedge, such as a 4-foot level, to make sure the door jambs are straight. They should be straight over their entire length and securely fastened to the rough framing members.

If the jambs are not secured, fasten them by inserting shims from opposite directions between the jamb and the rough framing, then drive 12d finish nails through the jambs and shims into the rough framing. If previous nailing has pulled a portion of the jamb out of alignment, pry it straight with a crowbar or a hammer with a fiberglass or steel handle. Reset shims behind the jamb and nail it with 12d nails.

**CABINET HEAD DOOR CASINGS**

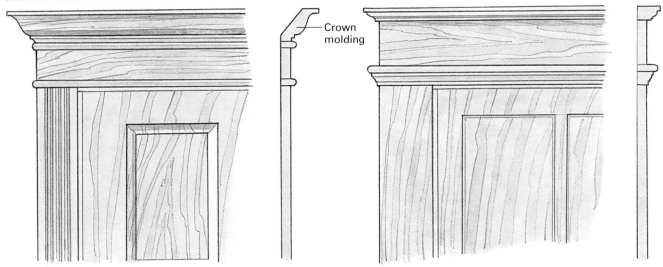

Crown molding

## INSTALLING MITERED CASINGS

Use a combination square to mark a ¼-inch reveal on the side and head jambs. Measure between the side reveals to determine the length of the head casing as measured heel to heel. Cut the head casing and tack it into position with a single 8d finish nail. Leave the nailhead exposed in case the head casing needs to be removed for trimming. Miter the side casings but leave them long. Position each casing upside down, with the toe of the miter against the floor. Be careful not to blunt the toe of the miter. Slide the casing against the head casing and mark where the toe of the head casing touches the side casing. Make a square cut at this mark. Using the reveal marks as guides, install the casings with 8d finish nails driven every 12 inches into the framing, and 4d nails driven every 12 inches into the window jambs. Always predrill at the ends of the casings. If the miters need trimming or adjustments, use the techniques described in Trim Joinery, page 40.

## INSTALLING BUTTED CASINGS

Mark the reveals on the edges of the jambs, using a combination square set to ¼ inch. Install the plinth blocks. Measure the distance from the top of the plinth blocks to the reveal for the head casing. Use this measurement to cut the side casings. Tack the side casings into position. Set the corner blocks atop the side casings with their inside lower corners just touching the intersection of the lines indicating the jamb reveals. Check to make sure the butt joints fit tightly and trim the casings if necessary. Tack the corner blocks into position. Measure and cut the head casing and check the fit—it should sit snugly between the corner blocks. Tack the head jamb into position. If you are satisfied with all the joints, install the casings with 8d finish nails driven every 12 inches into the framing, and 4d nails driven every 12 inches into the window jambs. Fasten the corner blocks with 8d finish nails driven into the rough framing.

## CABINET HEAD CASINGS

More elaborate head casings can be made of several pieces of moldings. The final design should be in keeping with the overall style and size of the room, and in harmony with the side casings—an elaborate head casing requires similarly ornate side casings. The installation techniques are similar to butted head casings. Instead of nailing up the pieces individually, build the cabinet head as a single unit, then install it as one piece. This ensures that the butt joints between the head and side casings are tight.

# BASEBOARDS

Baseboards are made in two basic styles—one-piece and built-up. One-piece baseboards are available at lumberyards and home improvement centers. They typically are 3 to 10 inches wide and feature a variety of profiles to match many architectural styles. A rule of thumb is to use baseboard 3 to 5 inches wide in rooms with 8-foot-high ceilings, baseboard 6 to 8 inches wide in rooms with 9- to 10-foot ceilings, and 10-inch or wider baseboard in rooms with taller ceilings. You'll find baseboard in paint-grade softwoods, such as pine, that are either unfinished or preprimed and ready for installation, and in finish-grade hardwoods, such as oak. One-piece baseboard is usually accompanied by a base shoe—a small, rounded-over piece of molding about ¾ inch high used to cover any gaps between the baseboard and the floor. Base shoe is not used if the floor covering is wall-to-wall carpet.

Built-up base molding is made of three or more pieces—a wide baseboard, a base shoe, and a cap, although it is possible to build a base out of any number of different moldings.

Installing a multipiece base molding is time-consuming and is usually reserved for rooms where highly decorative moldings are part of the overall architectural scheme. When designing elaborate baseboard moldings, be sure to plan how the base will meet the door casings.

As you work, select the best pieces of baseboard for the most conspicuous areas. Save lesser-quality pieces and cutoffs for out-of-the-way locations, such as closets.

## PLANNING THE INSTALLATION

Baseboard and other running moldings are the last moldings to be installed. Flooring should be complete, with doors, windows, and wainscoting already in place. Registers and baseboard heaters should be installed so that the baseboard can be run around them if necessary.

Three standard situations for molding installation are fitting a molding between two walls, from a wall to an outside corner, and between two outside corners. Each situation requires distinct joinery techniques. For best results, the process should proceed according to a set plan.

Installation should begin on the longest wall opposite the door, as shown in the illustration on the opposite page. This positions the first joints so that any imperfections are hidden from view, presenting the best workmanship to anyone entering the room.

The first piece of molding is butted into the corners at both ends. Cut the molding ¹⁄₁₆ inch long and back-cut or relieve the rear corner of each end. Put the molding into position. Because it's a bit long, you'll have to bow it slightly to get it to fit, then snap it into position against the wall. This action pushes the butted ends firmly into the corners. Don't force it; if the molding won't snap into position, trim it ¹⁄₃₂ inch and try again. From there, the work proceeds to either the right or left, continuing toward the door. When one side is finished, go back to the initial piece of molding and work in the opposite direction. Refer to the diagram at the top of the opposite page.

After the first piece is in place, look for any other walls that are not adjacent to the first wall and that have two inside corners. Cut and install base along these other walls, using butt joints at each end.

No matter which direction you work, the next piece of molding is coped to the first, using the coping techniques described in

Cutting a Coped Joint on page 40. The opposite end of this second piece is either butted to an inside corner or mitered for an outside corner. If you are working toward an inside corner, you'll need to measure precisely between the coped end and the butted end. Make the coped joint first, then cut the piece about ⅛ inch long, shaving small amounts from the end until you get a perfect fit. For out-of-square inside corners, simply adjust the coped joint by relieving the back of the molding.

If you are working toward an outside miter, cut the molding long. Fit the coped joint, then place the base into position and scribe the location of the wall corner on the back of the molding for cutting the outside miter.

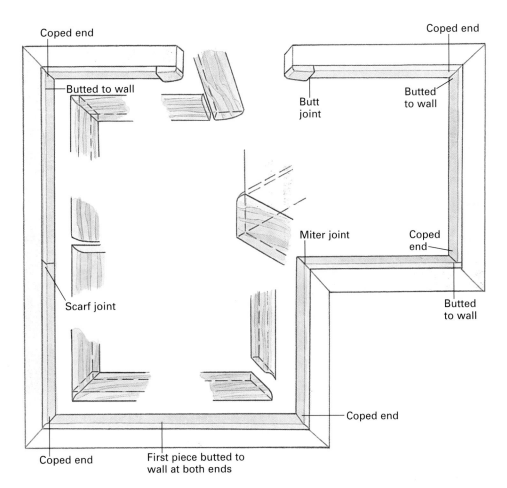

Coped end

Butted to wall

Coped end

Butt joint

Butted to wall

Miter joint

Coped end

Butted to wall

Scarf joint

Coped end

Coped end

First piece butted to wall at both ends

## CUTTING AN OUTSIDE MITER

Outside corners of walls rarely form an exact 90-degree angle. The easiest way to cut miters accurately is to gauge the angle of the corner with a bevel square, then use the blade of a power miter box like a protractor to measure the angle. Divide the angle by 2 to get your miter box setting for cutting. For example, if your corner measures 92 degrees, set your miter box to 46 degrees for cutting. If your miter box does not allow such precise settings, use small shims to angle the workpiece as described in Adjusting Miters on page 41. You won't have many chances to trim the miter on a piece that has the opposite end scribed to fit a coped joint—subsequent trimming will shorten the piece too much. Make your best cut on that piece, install it, and make any necessary adjustments on the next piece.

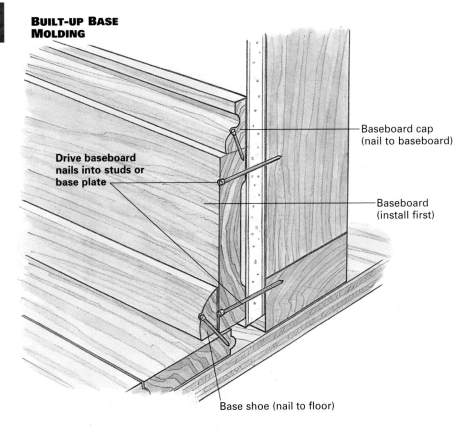

**BUILT-UP BASE MOLDING**

Baseboard cap (nail to baseboard)

**Drive baseboard nails into studs or base plate**

Baseboard (install first)

Base shoe (nail to floor)

## BASEBOARDS
*continued*

### NAILING BASE MOLDINGS

Baseboard is nailed into the bottom plate with two 8d nails driven every 16 inches. If the molding is taller than 4 inches, locate the studs and drive the uppermost nail into the stud framing. Predrill and nail the molding into corner framing.

The base shoe covers any gaps between the baseboard and the floor. The base shoe should be nailed into the floor rather than the baseboard, so that if the baseboard shrinks or expands with seasonal changes in humidity, it won't pull the base shoe with it and create a gap. Nail the base shoe with 6d nails driven every 12 to 16 inches. Base shoe is small and delicate, so you should predrill holes for the nails. Nail caps to the top of the main piece of baseboard molding. The illustration on the

### INSTALLING MOLDINGS WITH SCREWS

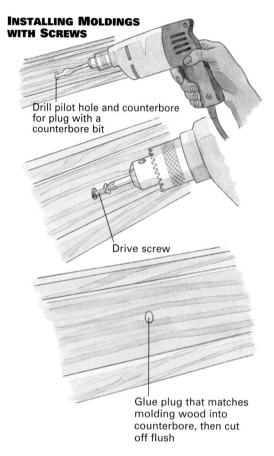

Drill pilot hole and counterbore for plug with a counterbore bit

Drive screw

Glue plug that matches molding wood into counterbore, then cut off flush

bottom of page 69 shows the nailing scheme.

When using an air nailer, be sure to hold the molding tight to the wall before pulling the trigger. Unlike a hand-driven nail, a nail driven by an air nailer will not draw workpieces together completely.

### SCRIBING BASE MOLDINGS

If a base shoe is not part of your baseboard plan and floors are uneven, scribe the bottom of the baseboard for a better fit. Run a pencil along the floor to transfer irregularities to the baseboard, then trim the baseboard with a hand plane. You can also scribe the ends of butt joints vertically to make them fit out-of-plumb walls.

### ENDING BASEBOARDS AT CASINGS AND PLINTHS

Make a good-looking end for a baseboard where it meets door casings or plinths. If the casing or plinth is thick enough, you'll be able to butt the baseboard directly to it for a good-looking joint. If not, try one of these methods:

■ If the base shoe is the only part that protrudes beyond the casings, then end it with a 30- to 45-degree bevel.

**SCRIBING A BASEBOARD**

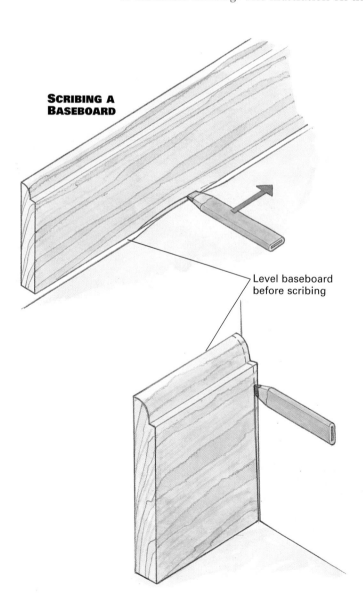

Level baseboard before scribing

## USING A PREACHER

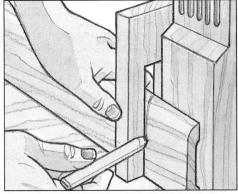

A preacher is a handy, easy-to-make jig for accurately scribing base molding to a door casing or plinth. Presumably, the jig is called a preacher because it always tells the truth.

Make a preacher from a scrap piece of ¾-inch pine or plywood. Cut a notch in the wood slightly wider and taller than your baseboard to form a U-shape. Cut the proper joint in the opposite end of the baseboard molding and place it in position—running past the casing. Fit the preacher over the baseboard and hold it firmly to the edge of the casing. The outside leg of the preacher is exactly in line with the casing and provides a straight surface for marking a cutting line across the face of the base molding; no measuring is necessary.

## PRO ADVICE: MAKING MITER CUTS

To cut miters in baseboard molding wider than 6 inches, use either a sliding compound miter saw or a table saw. With a compound miter saw, first tilt the blade to 45 degrees. Then position the piece flat on the bed of the tool and draw the blade across it to cut the miter. This method works well, but the sliding compound miter saw is expensive; you can rent one at your local rental dealer.

To cut a miter on a table saw, remove the fence and tilt the blade to 45 degrees. Place the piece of molding against the sliding miter gauge and push it into the blade to cut it. Large pieces of molding are awkward and difficult to secure to the sliding miter gauge and tend to wobble during cutting, ruining the miter. Have someone help support the end of long pieces of molding during cutting, and use a miter gauge with a built-in clamp, if possible.

■ If the entire profile of the baseboard is thicker than the casing, end it with a return miter. You can miter vertically, so the joint is virtually hidden and the end has a detailed finish, or across the face of the baseboard, so that it appears to turn into the floor.

■ If possible, butt the main section of a multipiece molding into the casing but miter the cap and run it all the way around the door frame, as shown on page 66. This also is a good way to end baseboards at vent openings and wall-mounted registers.

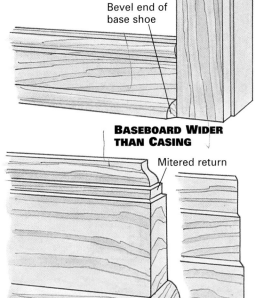

Bevel end of base shoe

**BASEBOARD WIDER THAN CASING**

Mitered return

Mitered corner wraps base shoe around mitered return

Length of mitered piece equals width of molding

Mitered turn to floor

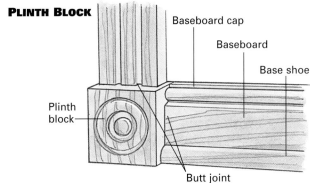

**PLINTH BLOCK**

Baseboard cap

Baseboard

Base shoe

Plinth block

Butt joint

# CHAIR AND PICTURE RAIL

Chair and picture rails are running moldings installed horizontally around the perimeter of a room. Both of these moldings originated for practical reasons, but today their use is mostly decorative.

**CHAIR RAIL:** This molding is installed on a wall about one-third the distance from the floor to the ceiling—usually 32 to 40 inches from the floor. Years ago, chair rail was used to protect plaster walls and wood paneling from being damaged by the backs of chairs and was usually found in dining rooms. Stock chair rail often has a symmetrical profile with a rounded bulge in its middle. Today, chair rail is primarily decorative, and is installed as a divider for a two-color wall scheme or as the cap for wallpaper "wainscoting" in any room of the house.

**PICTURE RAIL:** Popular during the late 19th century, this molding provided a way to hang artwork and mirrors without damaging plaster walls. The molding is formed with a thick ear designed to accept metal hooks. The hooks are attached to hanging wires for the art or mirror. The system allows the hanging items to be easily moved from one location to another without having to drill and screw new wall supports. Picture rails typically are installed high enough so that runs are not broken by window or door frames. For rooms with elaborate crown moldings, the picture rail usually is installed just under the crown and designed as part of the overall effect.

## INSTALLING CHAIR AND PICTURE RAILS

The methods for installing these types of moldings are similar to those used to install baseboard molding. At inside corners, the first piece of molding is butted and the next piece is joined with a coped joint. Outside corners have mitered ends.

To install the molding in an unfinished room, let 1×3 battens into the studs before the wallboard is installed. Batten backing ensures that you will be able to fasten the molding tight to the wall at any point. Use a chalk line to establish cut lines along the studs equal to the width of the battens. Set the blade of a circular saw to cut to the same depth as the thickness of the battens. Carefully cut each stud at the top and bottom of the lines, then make several parallel cuts inside the lines to relieve the waste. You can remove the waste quickly with a chisel. Install the battens—they should sit flush with the outside surface of the studs. Nail the battens with 8d common nails.

**SOME PICTURE RAIL STYLES**

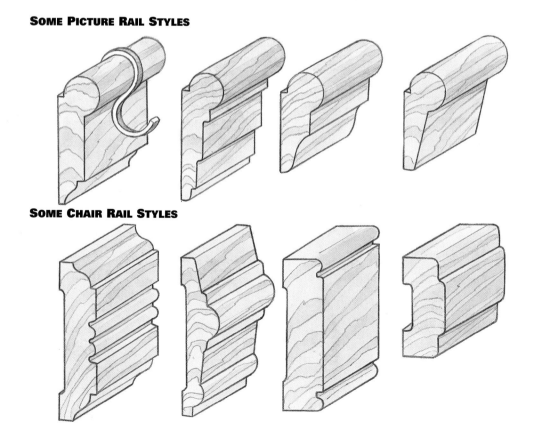

**SOME CHAIR RAIL STYLES**

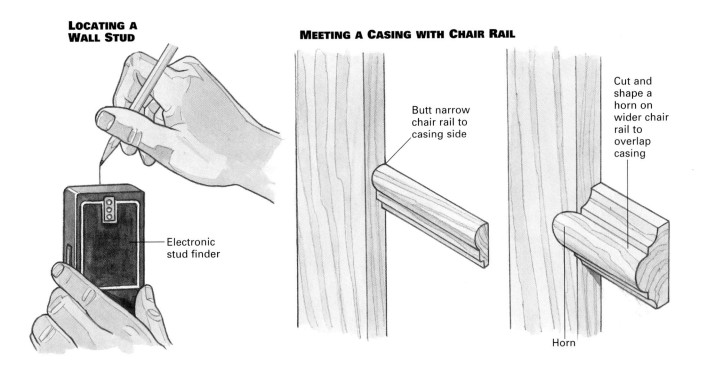

**LOCATING A WALL STUD**

Electronic stud finder

**MEETING A CASING WITH CHAIR RAIL**

Butt narrow chair rail to casing side

Cut and shape a horn on wider chair rail to overlap casing

Horn

If the wall finish is already in place, use a level to establish a guide line all the way around the room at the correct height for the rail. Use an electronic stud finder to locate the studs and mark their positions along the guide line. Determine an installation sequence, starting with the longest wall opposite the main doorway. The molding on this wall is butted on both ends. To ensure a tight fit, cut the molding long by $\frac{1}{16}$ inch, then relieve the back corners slightly. Fit the molding into position and snap it into place. Don't force it. If it is too long, trim the end and try again. Cope the next pieces of molding to fit, and continue around the room. Review the installation sequence illustration for baseboards shown on page 69.

Nail moldings with 8d finish nails driven into every stud. Picture rails must support considerable weight, so use pairs of 8d or 12d galvanized finish nails for better holding power. For maximum strength, use 2½-inch wood screws. Predrill for the screws with a counterbore bit, then fill the holes with wood plugs.

## MEETING CASINGS

The chair rail will probably meet door and window casings. If the rail is not as thick as the casings, then simply butt it. If the chair rail is thicker than the casing, notch a small horn to fit around the casing. Make the length of the horn ½ to ¾ inch long. If you prefer, cut a return miter for the rail as shown for baseboards on page 71.

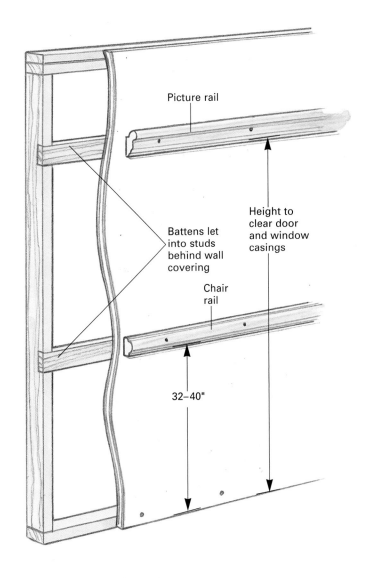

Picture rail

Battens let into studs behind wall covering

Height to clear door and window casings

Chair rail

32–40"

**Embossed designs on some crown moldings recall elaborately carved trim found in the grand mansions of the past.**

# CROWN MOLDING

Crown moldings bridge the intersection between the ceiling and the wall. They are prominent embellishments that provide even simple rooms with rich detail and character. Unlike other moldings that hide seams or protect wall surfaces, crown molding is strictly ornamental.

There are two types of crown moldings—flat and sprung. Flat moldings are applied flat against the wall, with their upper edges touching the ceiling. These types of moldings are rare, and usually are found in Arts and Crafts-style houses where a wide band of trim runs around the upper wall surface. Flat moldings require the same installation techniques as baseboard moldings, with butted and coped joints at inside corners and miters at outside corners.

Most crown moldings are sprung—they angle away from the wall, creating a hollow space behind the millwork. Typically, sprung moldings form a 45-degree angle, but a few types form different angles. Stock crown molding is available in solid paint- or finish-grade wood, veneered wood, and polyurethane. Most home improvement centers carry many styles and sizes of crown molding. Use molding 2 to 4 inches high (the vertical height of the installed molding) for 8-foot-tall ceilings, 4 to 6 inches high for 9-foot ceilings, and 6 to 10 inches high for ceilings that are 10 feet or more tall.

Built-up crowns combine flat and sprung molding, as shown on the opposite page. They may be as simple as a single piece of flat molding with a sprung molding nailed to it, or an elaborate combination of many individual pieces. This type of molding can be made up

## PRO ADVICE: CUTTING WIDE CROWNS

Wide crown molding is difficult to cut on a power miter box—the blade may not be large enough to cut all the way through the molding. However, a power miter box is an accurate tool for cutting angles. Use it to start your cut, lowering the blade as far as it will go. Stop the blade, and take the molding to the table saw. With the power off, raise the table-saw blade and use a combination of the blade tilt and the adjustable sliding miter gauge to position the table-saw blade precisely inside the kerf left by the miter box. When the piece is aligned, back it out of the blade area, start the saw, and finish the cut.

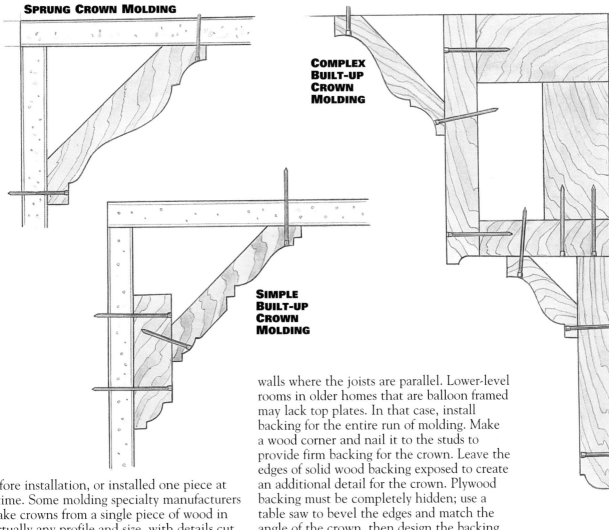

**SPRUNG CROWN MOLDING**

**COMPLEX BUILT-UP CROWN MOLDING**

**SIMPLE BUILT-UP CROWN MOLDING**

before installation, or installed one piece at a time. Some molding specialty manufacturers make crowns from a single piece of wood in virtually any profile and size, with details cut by a computer-controlled router or laser. This type of millwork is beautiful and expensive.

## INSTALLING CROWN MOLDING

Installing crown molding requires working overhead, typically from a ladder or a scaffold. Working in this position can be awkward, especially when trying to fit long pieces of molding. For best results, have someone help you. An air nailer is great for nailing crown because it allows one hand to be free for positioning and holding the molding in place.

Crown molding must be securely nailed to wall studs and ceiling joists.

Use an electronic stud finder to locate and mark all studs and joists. Where the ceiling joists run parallel to the wall, nail the bottom lip of the molding into the studs and drive a sufficiently long nail—a 12d or 16d finish nail—up through the main body of the molding at about a 45-degree angle to reach the top plate. If ceiling joists are exposed in an unfinished room, put blocking between the joists before installing the wallboard along

walls where the joists are parallel. Lower-level rooms in older homes that are balloon framed may lack top plates. In that case, install backing for the entire run of molding. Make a wood corner and nail it to the studs to provide firm backing for the crown. Leave the edges of solid wood backing exposed to create an additional detail for the crown. Plywood backing must be completely hidden; use a table saw to bevel the edges and match the angle of the crown, then design the backing so that it fits behind the molding (see the illustration on page 77).

Plan the installation sequence before you begin. Start on the longest wall opposite the door. Measure carefully, and cut the first piece $1/16$ inch long with butt cuts on both ends. Relieve the back of the cut to ensure a close fit. Bow the molding so that it fits into the corners and snap it into position. Don't force it; if the molding doesn't snap into position, trim $1/32$ inch from the length and try again.

After the first piece is in place, look for other walls not adjacent to the first wall that have two inside corners. Cut and install crown along these other walls, using butt joints at each end. Refer to the diagram on page 69 for the proper installation sequence.

# CROWN MOLDING
*continued*

**CHECKING WITH MOCK-UP JOINTS**

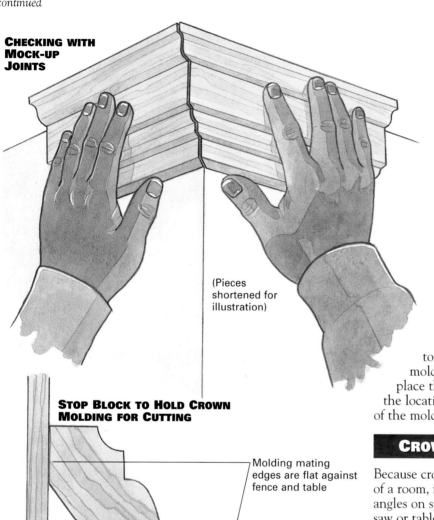

(Pieces shortened for illustration)

**STOP BLOCK TO HOLD CROWN MOLDING FOR CUTTING**

Molding mating edges are flat against fence and table

Stop block

Miter-saw fence

Miter-saw table

No matter which direction you work, the next piece of molding is coped to the first, using the coping techniques described in Cutting a Coped Joint on page 40. The opposite end of this second piece is either butted to an inside corner or mitered for an outside corner. If you are working toward an inside corner, you'll need to measure between the coped end and the butted end precisely. Make the coped joint first, then cut the piece about ⅛ inch long, shaving small amounts from the end until it fits perfectly. If you are working toward an outside miter, cut the molding long. Fit the coped joint, then place the crown into position and scribe the location of the wall corner on the back of the molding for cutting the miter.

## CROWN MOLDING JOINERY

Because crown molding is a prominent feature of a room, fine joinery is essential. Cutting angles on sprung moldings with a power miter saw or table saw is difficult; you must often hold the piece upside down and backwards, increasing chances for confusion. Always double check that your work is positioned properly before you make a cut so you won't waste molding.

To alleviate confusion when working with crown molding, make mock-up joints from scrap pieces of molding, as shown in the illustration above left. Use pieces about 3 feet long and make pairs of joints—a coped joint for inside corners and a mitered joint for outside corners. Refer to the pieces as you position your work for cutting. Where corners are not quite square, you can use your mock-up joints as a gauge for adjusting miters, trimming the ends as you would on the actual pieces until the fit is perfect. Then transfer the trim angles to your miter box for cutting the actual pieces.

When cutting crown with a power miter box, position the molding precisely with the upper and lower edges held flat to the table and fence of the tool. Clamp a piece of scrap wood to the saw table as a guide for positioning the molding correctly, as shown at left. Make sure long pieces are well supported beyond the miter box table.

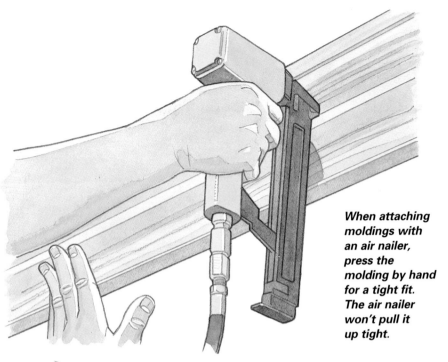

*When attaching moldings with an air nailer, press the molding by hand for a tight fit. The air nailer won't pull it up tight.*

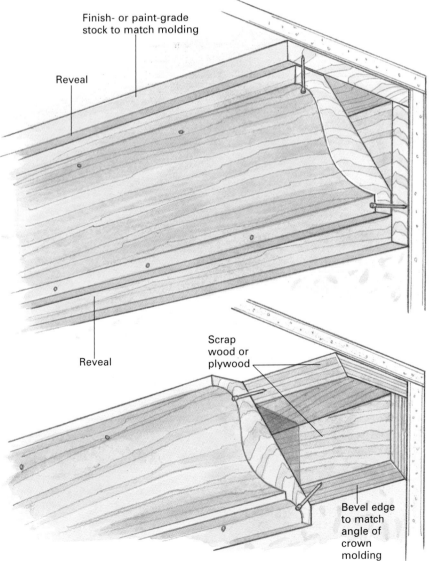

Finish- or paint-grade stock to match molding

Reveal

Reveal

Scrap wood or plywood

Bevel edge to match angle of crown molding

*When ceiling joists run parallel to the wall or in rooms where there is no top plate, provide nailers for crown moldings. One method is to nail finish- or paint-grade boards together into an L-shape, attach that to the wall studs, and nail the crown molding to it. Do this all around the room, and leave a reveal at both edges of the crown molding for better appearance. Another method is to assemble the L-shape support from scrap wood or plywood with the edges beveled to match the crown molding angle. The molding will cover this support and fit tightly against the ceiling and wall, so you can do this only on the walls that need it.*

# ADDING BEAUTY AND FUNCTION

You can add style and practicality to your home with finish carpentry skills. Such permanently attached improvements increase your home's value.

This section guides you through the design and construction of classic embellishments— a box-beam ceiling, fireplace mantel and surround, built-in shelving, and built-in closet organizers. Study the section on finishing to learn techniques that will complete all of your projects.

The projects in this section have step-by-step instructions; you may want to modify certain portions to create looks that are in keeping with your home's style.

**Finish carpentry embraces the beautiful, such as the boxed beams and fireplace surround on the opposite page, and the practical, such as the well-organized closet at left.**

# BOX BEAM

*An elegant coffered ceiling, with deep beams and recessed panels, is easy to simulate with box beams and moldings on a flat ceiling. Make sure your beams will leave enough headroom.*

A box-beam ceiling adds a touch of elegance to any room. Box-beam ceilings are usually found in more formal areas, such as living rooms, dining rooms, studies, and family rooms or great-rooms. Because a box-beam ceiling effectively lowers the height of a ceiling, it looks best in rooms with a ceiling 9 feet or higher. Most building codes require at least 84 inches of clearance for headroom.

Make box beams out of finish- or paint-grade material. Plywood is sturdy and stable, but the design shown here calls for the lower edges of the beam sides to be exposed, and plywood edges are unattractive. You can use plywood for the bottoms of the beams and solid wood for sides. The beams can be any size, but use modular dimensions based on standard framing material—2×4s or 2×6s.

## DESIGN AND LAYOUT

Start by laying out your design. Make a scale drawing of your ceiling, then make a grid pattern for the beams. Try to keep the rectangles of the pattern evenly spaced. There's no need to run a full-width beam at walls. Instead, use a single 1× board that matches the finished depth of your beam. Apply your molding to this board to complete the decorative portion of your grid.

When you're satisfied with the design, transfer the pattern to your ceiling by snapping chalk lines to indicate the position of the beam framing. The chalk lines will be 3½ inches apart for 2×4s, and 5½ inches apart for 2×6s. Next, use an electronic stud finder to locate the ceiling joists and mark their location on the grid. The first layer of framing is applied in one direction—perpendicular to the joists. Because a single piece of wood is stronger than two or more pieces installed end to end, use the longest pieces of lumber possible. At each joist secure the framing with two countersunk wood screws driven at least 1½ inches into the joist.

The second layer of framing material is installed perpendicular to the first, using the grid pattern as a guide. Secure this layer to the first with construction adhesive and countersunk wood screws 2½ inches long. If two layers of framing are the final depth of your beam, fill in the remaining areas with blocking. However, if your design calls for framing that is three layers deep, the last layer attached to the original layer should be separated by blocks—not solid lumber—to reduce the overall weight of the installation. Use blocks about 8 inches long installed every 2 feet. Secure the blocks with countersunk wood screws and construction adhesive. Predrill the blocks so they won't split.

## WRAPPING THE FRAMING

Wrap the framing with 1× material. For a clean-looking installation, set the bottom into grooves cut into the sides. Make the groove like a dado joint with a router and a straight bit, or a table saw with a dado blade. Make test cuts on scrap lumber to ensure the joint fits snugly—but not so snugly that you'll have to wrestle the pieces into position.

Precise measuring of all parts is critical. A typical groove for this type of construction is ¼ inch deep, so the bottom board will extend beyond the framing by ¼ inch on both sides. However, it's not necessary to make the bottom absolutely tight-fitting. Allow some play by undercutting the width of the bottom piece by ⅛ inch. For 2×4 framing, cut your bottom piece 3⅞ inches wide. For 2×6 framing, cut it 5⅞ inches wide. Note that framing materials can vary in width. Before you begin, measure the width of your framing materials; cut the parts to fit exactly.

Use a set pattern to wrap your beams with finish material. Start in one direction and complete all parallel beams, then finish the perpendicular ones. That way, all the butt

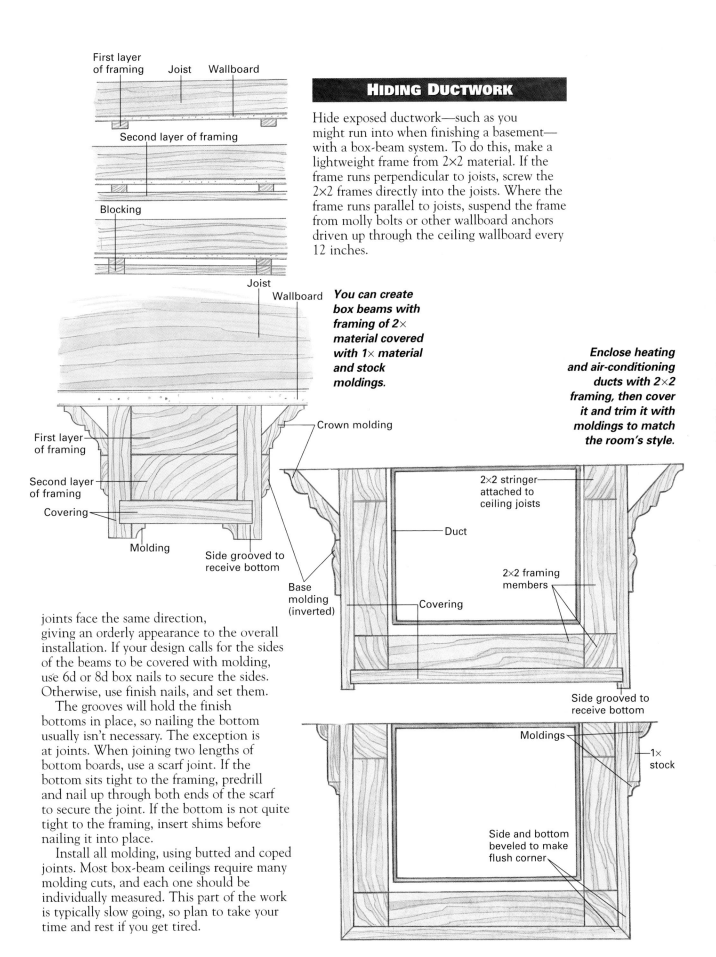

First layer of framing    Joist    Wallboard

Second layer of framing

Blocking

Joist

Wallboard

First layer of framing

Second layer of framing

Covering

Molding

Side grooved to receive bottom

*You can create box beams with framing of 2× material covered with 1× material and stock moldings.*

## HIDING DUCTWORK

Hide exposed ductwork—such as you might run into when finishing a basement—with a box-beam system. To do this, make a lightweight frame from 2×2 material. If the frame runs perpendicular to joists, screw the 2×2 frames directly into the joists. Where the frame runs parallel to joists, suspend the frame from molly bolts or other wallboard anchors driven up through the ceiling wallboard every 12 inches.

*Enclose heating and air-conditioning ducts with 2×2 framing, then cover it and trim it with moldings to match the room's style.*

Crown molding

Base molding (inverted)

2×2 stringer attached to ceiling joists

Duct

2×2 framing members

Covering

Side grooved to receive bottom

Moldings

1× stock

Side and bottom beveled to make flush corner

joints face the same direction, giving an orderly appearance to the overall installation. If your design calls for the sides of the beams to be covered with molding, use 6d or 8d box nails to secure the sides. Otherwise, use finish nails, and set them.

The grooves will hold the finish bottoms in place, so nailing the bottom usually isn't necessary. The exception is at joints. When joining two lengths of bottom boards, use a scarf joint. If the bottom sits tight to the framing, predrill and nail up through both ends of the scarf to secure the joint. If the bottom is not quite tight to the framing, insert shims before nailing it into place.

Install all molding, using butted and coped joints. Most box-beam ceilings require many molding cuts, and each one should be individually measured. This part of the work is typically slow going, so plan to take your time and rest if you get tired.

# FIREPLACE SURROUND

**Boards and stock moldings make up this fireplace surround and mantel. You can build it out of sheet goods, such as medium-density fiberboard, for a paint-grade installation. Basic joinery makes construction easy.**

A fireplace surround adds elegance and style. This one is a good project for a homeowner with moderate finish carpentry skills.

Make the surround with finish- or paint-grade material. For finish grade, try oak, cherry, or mahogany. Cherry and mahogany are medium-density woods that are somewhat easier to cut and work than oak. Under a natural finish, cherry and mahogany have a rich red color that slowly darkens with age. Oak has a medium tan color.

For paint-grade material, use plywood or medium-density fiberboard for the flat surfaces. Both materials are easy to cut, shape, and paint. They cost less than half of what hardwood costs.

Add detail and character to your surround with applied moldings. Copy the patterns shown in these photos or create your own. You can buy fanciful carvings—actually precut, embossed pieces of hardwood—in many styles and sizes at home improvement centers. Attach them with epoxy glue and small brads. Because it is difficult to match the grain of these applied decorations to the wood used for the main body of the surround, they are not recommended for finish-grade projects. However, they work well with paint-grade materials.

## DETERMINING SIZE

The size of the surround depends on the size of your fireplace opening. Most building codes require that combustible materials surrounding a fireplace opening must allow 1 inch of clearance for each $\frac{1}{8}$ inch they project out from the face of the fireplace, to a distance of 12 inches. For example, wood molding $\frac{3}{4}$ inch thick cannot be installed closer than 6 inches to the fireplace opening. Wood molding $1\frac{1}{2}$ inches thick cannot be closer than 12 inches to the opening. Some codes forbid any combustible materials within 8 inches of the opening. Check with your local building department for the exact

## PRO ADVICE:
## PLANE AWAY SAW MARKS

Ripping pieces of wood on the table saw leaves saw marks on the edges. Add an extra $\frac{1}{16}$ inch to the width of the piece, then place the piece in a vise and remove blade marks with a hand plane. A jointer—a power tool—makes this job even easier.

## MATERIALS

| Part | T | W | L | Mat | Amt. |
|------|---|---|---|-----|------|
| A Pilaster front | ¾" | 8¼" | * | SS | 2 |
| B Pilaster side | ¾" | 5½" | * | SS | 2 |
| C Pilaster side | ¾" | 5½" | * | SS | 2 |
| D Bridge front | ¾" | 12⅝" | * | SS | 1 |
| E Bridge bottom | ¾" | 4¾" | * | SS | 1 |
| F Base molding | ¾" | 7½" | * | SS | 6 |
| G Molding | ½" | ⅜" | * | SS | 6 |
| H Molding | ⅜" | ⅝" | * | SS | 18 |
| I Molding | ⅜" | ¾" | * | SS | 7 |
| J Filler | ¾" | 2⅞" | * | SW | 5 |
| K Molding | ¾" | ¾" | * | SS | 7 |
| L Cove Molding | 2¼" | 4½" | * | SS | 7 |
| M Mantel | 1½" | 10⅞" | * | SS | 1 |

*\* To fit opening; see instructions*

**Materials Key:** *SS–solid stock of choice; SW–scrapwood. For a painted surround, substitute medium-density fiberboard for parts A–E.*

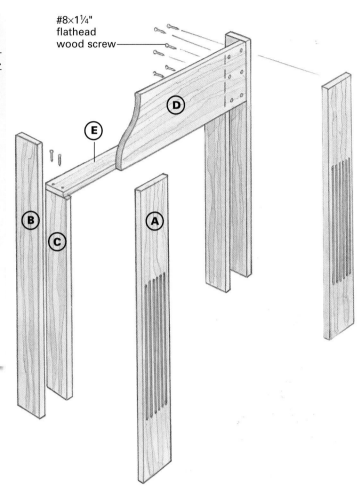

#8×1¼" flathead wood screw

specifications in your area, then determine the inside dimensions of your surround. Plan to cover the space between the surround and the fireplace opening with noncombustible materials such as ceramic tile.

### MAKING THE PARTS

Build the fireplace surround as a unit, then mount it to the wall. If possible, clear a large enough space to permit assembly of the entire unit—a raised worktable is ideal.

Use the materials list at the bottom of the page to determine the width of the pieces; length depends on the size of your fireplace opening. Once you know the size of the opening and the amount of clearance required by local building codes, fill in the lengths on the chart.

First build the inside of the box with parts C and E. Notice that part E, the bridge bottom, is ¾ inch narrower than the the pilaster sides (C). During assembly, the backs of these pieces are held flush so that when the bridge front, part D, is applied, the front edges of the inside box and the front of the bridge are flush.

The pilaster fronts (A) run up the front of this assembly to form a slight bump-out detail. The sum of the inside of the box, measured vertically, and the width of the bridge front determines the length of the pilaster fronts (A) and the pilaster sides (B). Rip the pilaster fronts (A) to 8¼ inches wide. Cut them to length. Rip the pilaster sides (B) 5½ inches wide, and cut them to length.

### FLUTING THE PILASTERS

For a decorative detail, add grooves called flutes to the front of the pilasters. Make the grooves with a router secured in a router table. Equip the router with a ½-inch round-nose bit; set the router to make the flutes ¼ inch deep. Plan the design carefully so that the flutes are centered in the pilaster front. Draw lines across the back of the pilasters exactly where the flutes start and where they end. Use these lines as guides to make sure the tops and bottoms of the flutes will be aligned perfectly. Draw a vertical line across the front of the router table fence to indicate where to start and stop the routing.

# FIREPLACE SURROUND
*continued*

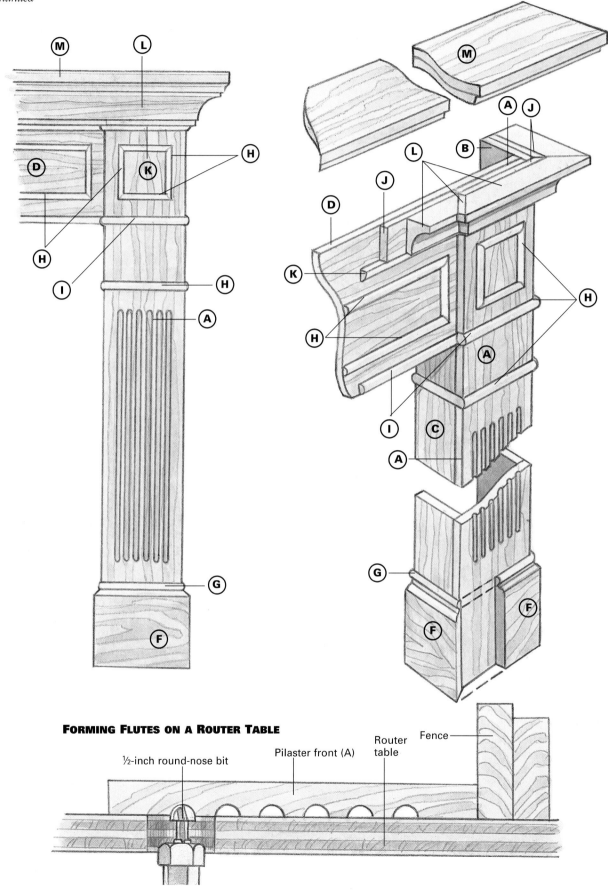

**FORMING FLUTES ON A ROUTER TABLE**

½-inch round-nose bit

Pilaster front (A)

Router table

Fence

The flutes should be evenly spaced 1 inch apart, measured on center. To ensure the flutes are cut correctly, mark the proper fence locations on the table on each side of the router bit. After each cut, reposition the fence according to the marks. Once you've established guide lines and layout marks, test the setup on a piece of scrap wood cut to the same dimensions as the pilaster. When you're satisfied, cut the flutes in the workpieces.

To rout a flute, set the fence, grip the workpiece firmly, line up the starting guide mark, and start the router. Lower the part decisively onto the router bit. Immediately guide the pilaster along the fence to the stop mark, then lift it off the bit. Make the cut in one motion—hesitation may burn the inside of the flute.

## ASSEMBLY

Assemble the parts as shown in the illustration on page 83. Use 2-inch flathead wood screws for joints that won't show. Where joints will show, fasten the parts with 6d finish nails and glue. Attach the pilaster sides (C) to the bridge bottom (E) with wood screws and glue. Attach the bridge front (D) to the edge of the bridge bottom and the pilaster sides (B) with 6d nails and glue. Attach the pilaster fronts (A) to the pilaster sides with 6d nails and glue. Secure the pilaster fronts to the bridge front by driving 1¼-inch-long wood screws through the back of the bridge front into the pilaster. Clamp the pilaster fronts tightly to the bridge front to make sure the screws don't force apart the joint. Make sure all joints are tight and the unit is square. Set the assembly aside to allow the glue to dry.

## ADDING MOLDING DETAILS

Cut and apply all the molding as shown in the illustrations, using the molding specifications listed in the materials list. You can create any details of your own. Miter end joints, and miter the edges of wide details such as the base molding (F). For best appearance, glue the pieces to the surround and clamp them until the glue is dry. To ensure that the mantel fits tightly to the wall, don't install it or the cove molding until the main body of the surround unit is in place.

## ATTACHING THE SURROUND

Fasten the surround to wall-mounted cleats. Rip 2×8s to fit snugly into the hollow space inside the pilasters. Measure the distance

---

### PRO ADVICE: CUTTING SMALL MOLDINGS

When using a power miter box to cut miters in thin pieces of molding, such as the ⅜-inch wide material specified for this project, it can be difficult to see your marks. Try marking the miter locations with a combination square and a pencil with a fine point, then cut the miters by hand using a dovetail saw. Clamp the workpieces securely when cutting by hand.

between the pilasters carefully and mount the cleats in position. Screw the cleats to the wall framing. If you can't find studs, secure the cleats with hollow-wall fasteners and construction adhesive. Place the surround into position and nail it to the cleats with 6d finish nails. Scribe the back of the mantel to the wall if necessary, and cut it to fit. Then apply the cove molding or a standard crown molding to the underside of the mantel, using 6d finish nails. Miter outside corners and use butted and coped joints for inside corners.

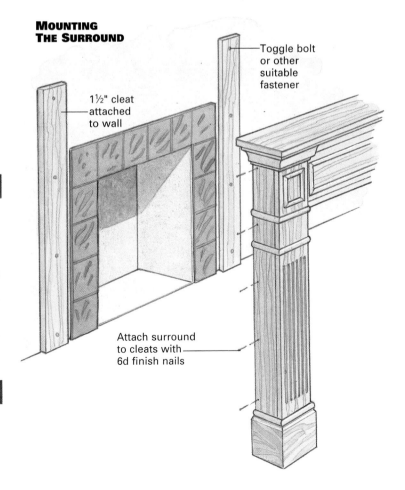

**MOUNTING THE SURROUND**

Toggle bolt or other suitable fastener

1½" cleat attached to wall

Attach surround to cleats with 6d finish nails

# SHELVES

Built-in shelving is always an attractive addition. Shelving puts walls to good use, adds valuable storage space, and provides room for many smaller, individual items such as books or decorative knickknacks. Carefully constructed shelving blends with a home's style and, because it is a permanent fixture, adds to the value of your house. Built-in units are attached to framing members, making them exceptionally strong. They can be installed anywhere you have adequate room, and they are an especially good way to convert alcoves or out-of-the-way niches into usable storage areas.

There are two types of built-in shelving—open and closed. Open shelves are hung on wall brackets and have no back or end panels. The openness of this design makes it ideal for displaying collectibles. The shelves are usually supported by adjustable brackets, so rearranging them is easy.

**BUILT-IN BOOKCASE CONSTRUCTION**

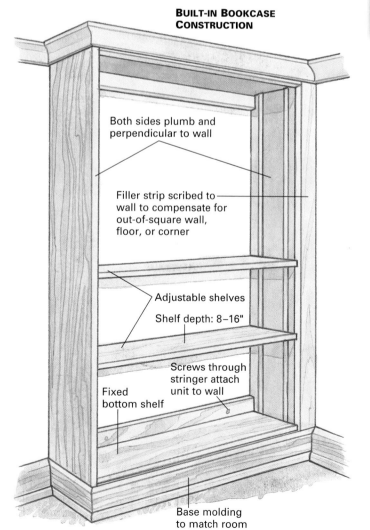

Both sides plumb and perpendicular to wall

Filler strip scribed to wall to compensate for out-of-square wall, floor, or corner

Adjustable shelves

Shelf depth: 8–16"

Fixed bottom shelf

Screws through stringer attach unit to wall

Base molding to match room

Closed shelves have backs and sides, and are often trimmed with the same baseboard and crown moldings that run around the perimeter of the room. Closed shelves provide a sheltering place for delicate or fragile items and have a greater weight-bearing capacity than open shelving. Closed shelves can be constructed as freestanding bookcases like the one shown above. Well-designed and constructed closed shelving requires many of the same techniques used to make fine furniture. However, building closed units is well within the abilities of a finish carpenter with moderate skills.

## PLANNING SHELF USE

The size and style of the shelves you build depends on how you plan to use them. Stacks of books are heavy but don't require much depth. Stereo equipment isn't too heavy but stackable components usually require lots of space. Use these general guidelines:

■ A running foot of shelf space holds 8 to 10 regular books. Estimate 10 to 12 children's books per foot and 4 to 5 large reference books, such as a dictionary, per foot.
■ Stackable stereo components measure about 18 inches wide and 14 inches deep. If you will stack the components, measure the total vertical height of your system. Most systems have lots of power cords and speaker

wires that make open shelves look messy. Plan for closed shelves. If possible, inset the back of the unit 1 inch, leaving a hollow space for cords and wires. To provide clearance for plugs, drill 1¼-inch-diameter holes in the back.

■ The arrangement of shelves that will hold collectibles depends on the height, width, and depth of the individual pieces. A standard shelf depth of 12 inches provides adequate room for many different kinds of knickknacks, giving you the flexibility to alter arrangements as your collections change. If you are an avid collector, plan extra room for your collection to grow.

## SHELVING SPANS

Different shelf materials have different span limits. A span limit is the distance between supports that a shelf can span before it bends appreciably or breaks. To determine shelf spans, architects use a weight standard based on books—25 pounds per cubic foot (see the illustration at right). Hardwood and plywood are suitable for longer shelves, while glass and particleboard shelves must be kept short. Although hardwood is stronger than plywood of the same thickness, changes in humidity can cause it to bend or twist. Plywood is more stable, but you'll need to cover exposed edges with veneer tape.

Shelf material can be strengthened with reinforcement, adding up to 40 percent to the span limit. Doubling the thickness of the material is one solution. Another is to stiffen the shelf by adding aprons or edge banding, as shown in the illustration on page 89. Aprons are small pieces of wood, usually wider than they are thick, that are nailed or screwed on edge to the bottom of the shelf. Edge banding is applied to the front of the shelf. It can be applied directly with finish nails and glue, or it can be rabbeted so that the shelf sits inside a groove. Edge banding is a good way to cover the edges of plywood shelves while adding strength. For glass or acrylic shelves, slip aluminum channels over the edges.

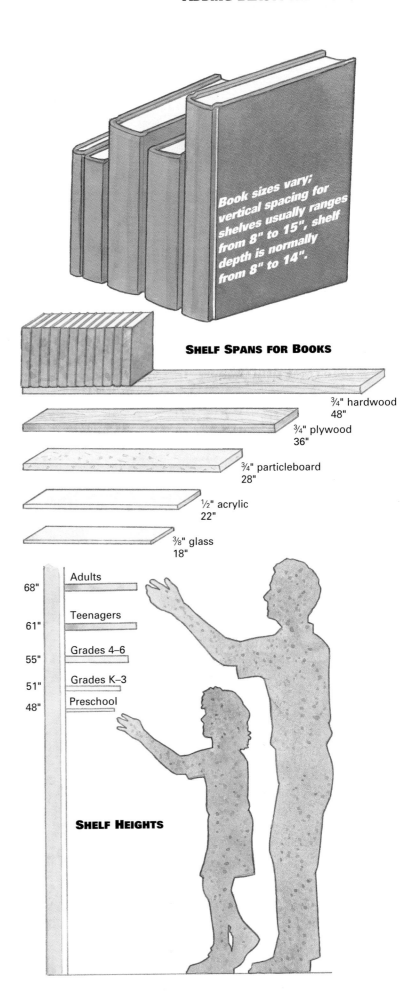

Book sizes vary; vertical spacing for shelves usually ranges from 8" to 15", shelf depth is normally from 8" to 14".

**SHELF SPANS FOR BOOKS**

¾" hardwood
48"

¾" plywood
36"

¾" particleboard
28"

½" acrylic
22"

⅜" glass
18"

**SHELF HEIGHTS**

68" — Adults

61" — Teenagers

55" — Grades 4–6

51" — Grades K–3

48" — Preschool

## SHELVES
*continued*

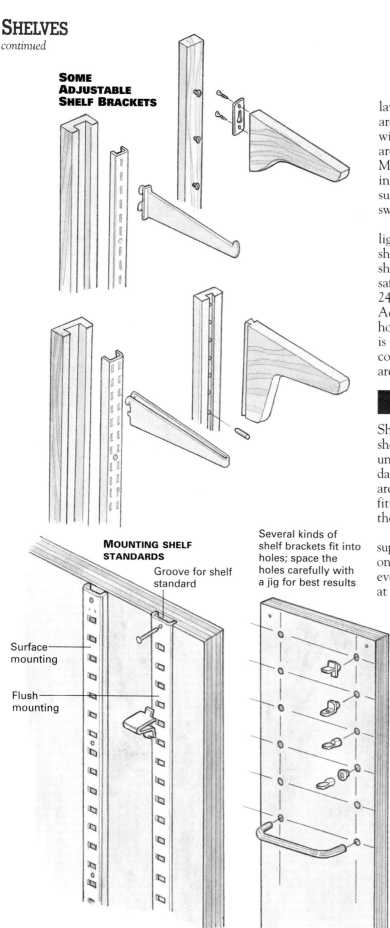

**SOME ADJUSTABLE SHELF BRACKETS**

**MOUNTING SHELF STANDARDS**

Groove for shelf standard

Surface mounting

Flush mounting

Several kinds of shelf brackets fit into holes; space the holes carefully with a jig for best results

Particleboard shelves covered with a thin layer of laminated plastic called melamine are available in many standard lengths and widths at home improvement centers. They are an excellent low-cost option for shelving. Medium-density fiberboard is another inexpensive choice for painted shelves. Be sure to use an oil-based primer; a latex primer swells the fibers, weakening the material.

For display shelves, glass or clear acrylic lets light through from all angles. Glass shelving should be at least ⅜ inch thick and the edges should be rounded over to make the shelves safer and easier to handle. For spans 18 to 24 inches long, use ½-inch-thick glass. Acrylic is a good alternative to glass if the household includes small children and safety is a concern. Acrylic scratches easily and costs as much as glass. Acrylic shelves that are ½ inch thick will span up to 22 inches.

### SUPPORTING SHELVES

Shelves are either fixed or adjustable. Fixed shelves typically are found on closed shelving units, and the ends of the shelves fit into dado grooves cut in the sides. Fixed shelves are strong and gain added stiffness from being fitted into dadoes, but once they are attached they can't change position.

Adjustable shelves in open units are supported by adjustable brackets that hang on metal standards—long metal strips with evenly spaced holes that can hold brackets at various heights. The standards usually are attached to decorative wood strips that are screwed into wall framing. This requires you to locate the wall studs and plan your shelf layout to have standards installed on 16- or 32-inch centers. Cut a groove in each wood strip and set the standard into it to partially hide it. You can use standard metal brackets or make them yourself from hardwood fitted with keyhole hangers. By installing several standards on a wall, you can vary the length and position of each shelf to create interesting patterns.

Adjustable shelves in closed units are supported at the ends by metal standards and movable clips, or with shelf supports that have pegs that fit into holes drilled at regular intervals along the ends of the unit. Face the front edges of the ends with strips of wood to hide the hardware.

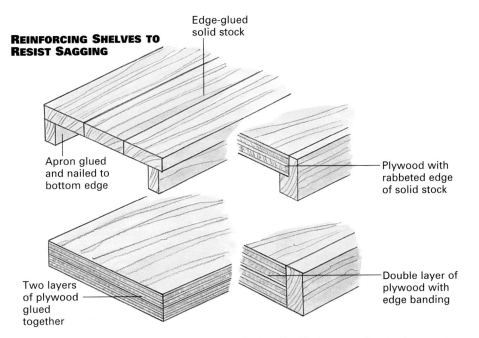

**REINFORCING SHELVES TO RESIST SAGGING**

Edge-glued solid stock

Apron glued and nailed to bottom edge

Plywood with rabbeted edge of solid stock

Two layers of plywood glued together

Double layer of plywood with edge banding

If you use glass or acrylic shelving, use clips or pegs made of plastic or vinyl to prevent the shelf material from being scratched. Also, keep in mind these points:

■ Consider who will use the shelves. Most adults can easily reach a height of 68 inches from the floor, but shelves for preschoolers shouldn't be more than 48 inches high (see the illustration on page 87).

■ Add a mirrored back or sides to display shelving to give the illusion of depth, provide more light, and permit views of the backs of particularly interesting items. Buy mirrored glass cut to your specifications, or use mirrored acrylic sheets, available at home improvement centers.

■ Add small, recessed lights to highlight certain items and to provide illumination at night. Choose from standard 110-volt or low-voltage fixtures.

## WALL-HUNG SHELVES

Open shelves provide storage and display space without the complicated installation of built-in shelves or the mass of a bookcase. Fixed shelves are easily installed with commercial metal hardware or decorative wooden brackets. Hardware stores and home improvement centers carry a range of wall-mount shelf standards and adjustable brackets for more versatility. If you need a number of shelves on a wall, installing standards and adjustable brackets is the easiest method, even if you don't need the shelves to be movable.

To mount brackets for a fixed shelf or standards for adjustable brackets, first locate the wall studs behind the proposed shelf location. Mark the location for the shelf. Then, screw the first bracket or standard to the wall with 2-inch screws of suitable diameter. Hold the next bracket or standard against the wall at the next location, and lay a level across the brackets. (Span the brackets with a straightedge to lay the level on, if necessary.) For shelf standards, insert brackets in corresponding locations and put the level across them. When the brackets are level, screw the second one to the wall. Repeat for additional brackets or standards.

Some small decorative shelves are made to attach to the wallboard itself. Follow manufacturer's load recommendations for these and other brackets.

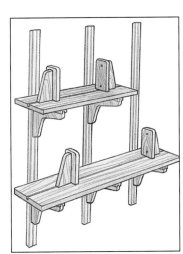

# CLOSETS

Build an organizer to make better use of closet space. Readily accessible shelves, pullout bins, and multilevel poles for hanging garments of various lengths ensure that all of the closet space is put to good use. You can make this mostly hidden organizer from low-cost, paint-grade materials.

## PLANNING

Plan your closet organizer by following these guidelines:

■ If you add lights and switches, you may need a building permit. Check with your local building department before you begin.

■ Clothes-hanger poles require at least 12 inches in front and behind. For hanging full-length garments, allow at least 64 inches from the top of the pole to the floor. For shirts, folded trousers, and other half-length items, allow 42 inches. A clothes pole longer than 4 feet must be supported at its center.

■ An average item of clothing requires 1 inch of horizontal space on a clothes pole. Bulky winter clothing requires 2 to 3 inches.

■ Place the highest closet shelf no more than 84 inches from the floor. This leaves about 1 foot of vertical space above the shelf for storage. Be sure that light fixtures are placed so that items on shelves cannot touch bulbs.

■ Place baskets or drawers in the middle of the closet so that front walls and doors don't get in their way.

## INSTALLING SHELVES

Installing a closet shelf isn't difficult, but cutting and fitting the shelf is often difficult because small closets usually are not square.

Shelves rest on cleats—1×3 or 1×4 boards that run along the back and sides of the closet. These cleats also provide solid backing for closet pole sockets.

Begin by marking a level line on the back and side walls of the closet to show where the bottom of the shelf and the top of the cleats will be. Use an electronic stud finder to locate the wall framing. Install the cleats with two 8d finish nails or two 2½-inch wallboard screws into each stud. Install the rear cleat first, and butt the side cleats to it to hide the joints. Measure out from the back wall and mark the shelf width along the side walls.

Check the rear corners with a framing square, as shown in the illustration below. Note which way the wall is skewed. Transfer your measurement to one end of the shelf material and cut the end to match the angle of the wall.

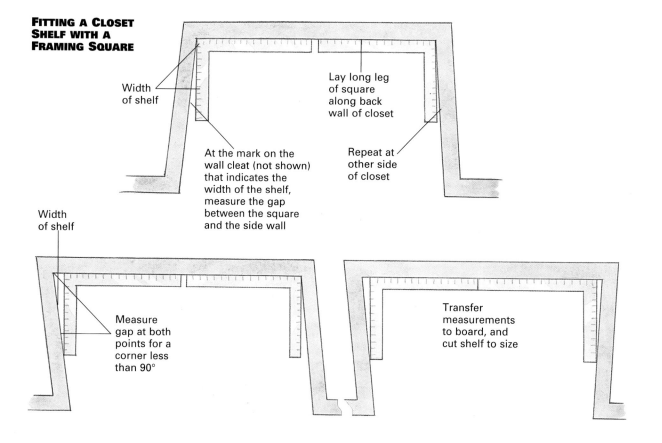

**FITTING A CLOSET SHELF WITH A FRAMING SQUARE**

Width of shelf

Lay long leg of square along back wall of closet

At the mark on the wall cleat (not shown) that indicates the width of the shelf, measure the gap between the square and the side wall

Repeat at other side of closet

Width of shelf

Measure gap at both points for a corner less than 90°

Transfer measurements to board, and cut shelf to size

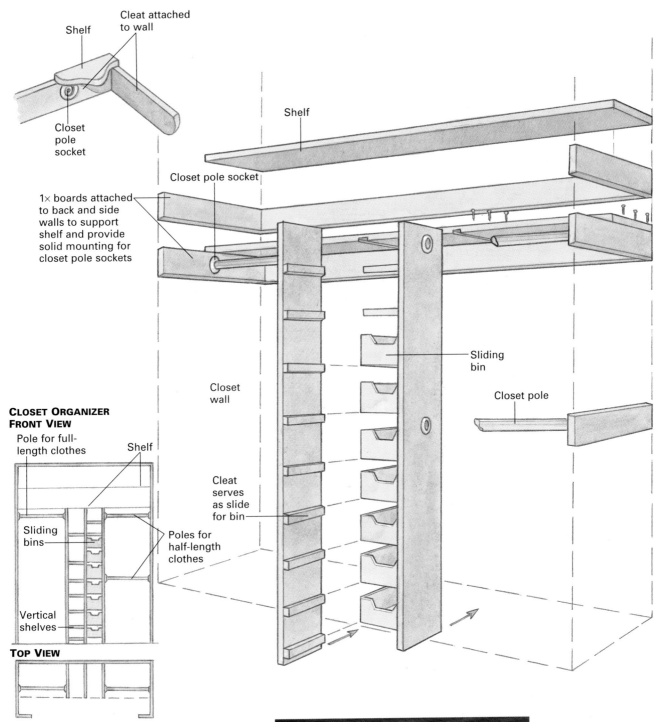

Shelf

Cleat attached to wall

Closet pole socket

Shelf

Closet pole socket

1× boards attached to back and side walls to support shelf and provide solid mounting for closet pole sockets

Sliding bin

Closet pole

Closet wall

**CLOSET ORGANIZER FRONT VIEW**

Pole for full-length clothes

Shelf

Cleat serves as slide for bin

Sliding bins

Poles for half-length clothes

Vertical shelves

**TOP VIEW**

Next, measure the total distance along the back edge of the cleats. On your shelf material, measure and mark this distance, starting from the corner of the trimmed end.

Check the opposite corner of the closet. Note which way the wall is skewed and measure any gaps. Transfer your measurements to the shelf material, using the mark that indicates the back corner of the closet as your starting point. Cut the shelf and fit it on top of the cleats. You may have to angle the shelf to get it to fit between out-of-square walls.

## MAKING VERTICAL SHELVES OR BINS

Home improvement centers carry modular storage systems that adapt easily to most closets. You can build your own, too.

If you decide to make your own bins or small vertical shelves, build them 1 foot wide. Install 1×2 cleats to hold shelves or slide-out bins, or inset metal adjustable shelf standards (see page 88). To ensure that cleats are installed parallel to each other, clamp shelf sides together when marking cleat locations and mark all pieces at the same time.

# FINISHING TECHNIQUES

*Careful preparation and application will ensure a finish that enhances your work.*

Proper finishing techniques ensure that your project looks great. The primary objective is to prepare smooth, blemish-free surfaces so that paint or clear finish adheres well.

## FILLING NAIL HOLES

Fill nail holes with latex- or acrylic-base putty or plastic wood fillers. Use putty for paint-grade work—it dries fast and is easy to sand. For finish-grade work, use colored wood fillers. A single piece of wood may have many color variations, so you'll need to buy several shades of filler to have a close color match.

Set all nailheads at least ⅛ inch below the surface to give putty or wood filler enough surface to adhere to or the putty might pop out. Use a nail set that's the right size for the nailhead.

Press the putty or filler into nail holes or small cracks with a thin, flexible putty knife. Scrape off any excess putty and allow to dry thoroughly before sanding with 150- or 220-grit sandpaper. Be careful not to oversand, removing surrounding wood

## THE ART OF CUTTING IN

Cutting in means creating a clean, straight edge with your paint stroke. Use cutting in techniques to paint the edges of trim or moldings without getting paint on adjacent walls. Holding the brush handle like a pencil, load up about ¼ of the length of the bristles with paint. Pause to let excess paint drip back into the paint can. Apply the tip of the brush against the trim surface, holding the bristles back from the edge about ½ inch. As you touch the trim, begin to draw the brush toward you, applying increasing pressure against the bristles to spread them, widening the brush stroke. Stop as the edge of the bristles contacts the outer edge of the trim. Continue drawing the brush to you until you need to refill the bristles. At this point, check the very beginning of your stroke. There should be a lip of excess paint at the point where you started. But because you began well back from the edge of the trim, this excess paint should not run onto adjacent surfaces. Use the tip of your brush to smooth this lip of paint, applying pressure and drawing the brush to you once again to create a sharply defined edge.

When cutting in, always work close to your body so you can see the edge of the paint easily. Don't overextend your reach; stop painting, and move your ladder.

and leaving a noticeable depression. Inspect the filled holes. Putty can shrink as it dries, leaving a slight depression that requires a second application.

## CAULKING PAINT-GRADE WORK

Open joints and gaps between millwork and wall or ceiling surfaces can be hidden with paintable caulk. Acrylic latex caulk is easy to apply, stays flexible, and cleans up with water. After the caulk is dry, it can be painted to match the woodwork.

Apply caulk with a tube-type caulk gun. Cut the end of the nozzle with a razor knife at about a 45-degree angle. Cut only the very tip to create a narrow bead—if the flow is too slow, carefully cut again to create a slightly larger hole. Place the cut side of the nozzle into the crack and squeeze the trigger as you move the gun, forcing the caulk into the gap to fill it. Work only one joint or gap at a time. When it has been filled, smooth the bead with a moistened fingertip to flatten the bead and force the caulk into any gaps. Wipe off excess caulk with a damp rag.

## FIXING HAMMER DENTS

Even the best finish carpenter occasionally dents a workpiece with the hammer head. In paint-grade work, dents are easy to fix. Drill one or two small (1/16-inch diameter) holes in the dent to anchor the putty. Spread putty over the dent and allow it to dry thoroughly, then sand the area smooth. It's better to underfill the dent and give it a second application of putty because when dry, putty can be hard—harder than the surrounding wood. When sanding a filled area, it's possible to sand away the surrounding, softer wood before the putty is sufficiently smoothed, adding another problem to the original one. Minimize the amount of sanding by building up the fill in stages.

Fixing dents in finish-grade work is more difficult. The best bet is to try to raise the dent. First, wet the dent with hot water. Then touch the tip of a preheated clothes iron to the dent to heat the water-soaked wood, causing it to swell. Once the dent is raised, let it dry and sand the area smooth.

## SANDING WOODWORK

Most woodwork requires minor touch-up sanding before paint or stain is applied. Use a medium-fine grit sandpaper, such as 150-grit, to remove any scratches, small imperfections, and raised grain. On detailed millwork, it's best to sand by hand, using light pressure and letting your fingers conform to the molding.

Sanding near joints, especially flat miters, requires care. Sand with the grain right to the edge of the joint. Don't lap over or you'll sand the adjoining surface across the grain, leaving scratch marks that are difficult to remove. If joints are not well-aligned, first shave the high side of the joint with a sharp chisel until it is nearly flush with the adjoining surface. Then sand both sides smooth.

When you're finished sanding, remove dust with a soft-bristle brush. Then, wipe the surfaces with a tack rag.

## PAINTING

Paint finish-carpentry projects with gloss or semigloss interior latex paint. Gloss paints are more durable than flat paint, are easier to clean, and resist scratching. Work in a clean, dust-free, moderately warm room.

Prime raw wood before painting. A primer fills open wood grain and creates an even surface that accepts paint evenly. If possible, prime all wood and millwork before it is installed. Let the primer dry for 24 hours, then sand all pieces lightly with 220-grit sandpaper to smooth raised grain. Spot-prime any bare wood or knots that show through the first primer coat. Let primed wood dry thoroughly before handling. Install the trim, set the nails, and fill nailholes and other imperfections. Sand putty or filler smooth, then spot-prime the sanded areas.

To paint installed trim, use top-quality brushes, such as China-bristle brushes. They are expensive, but with proper care they will provide years of excellent results. For trimwork, you'll need two brushes—a 2½- or 3-inch brush for large, flat areas, and a 2-inch sash brush for cutting in around moldings. A sash brush has a diagonally shaped tip to make cutting in easier and more precise.

Fill a clean, dry container with only as much paint as you can use in half an hour to 45 minutes of painting—about 1 quart is usually sufficient. That way, the paint you're using won't dry out and thicken. Cover the remaining paint tightly.

### PAINTING A TRADITIONAL DOUBLE-HUNG WINDOW

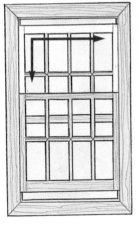

**1** Paint across, then down on the frame of the upper sash

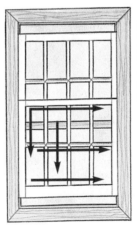

**3** Paint across, then down on the frame, bars, and muntins of the lower sash

**5** Paint down on the remaining bars and muntins on the upper sash

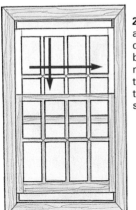

**2** Paint across, then down on the bars and muntins on the inside of the upper sash

**4** Push the lower sash up and pull the upper one down; paint across the bottom of the upper sash

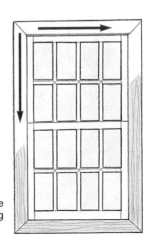

**6** Paint the casing

# FINISHING TECHNIQUES
*continued*

Professional painters cut in trim paint to adjacent surfaces, being careful not to overlap paint and wiping up mistakes immediately with a damp rag. (See The Art of Cutting In on page 92.) With a little practice, you should be able to cut in trim paint. However, you can prevent mistakes by masking off adjacent surfaces with tape. Always use painter's masking tape—it comes off without marring or pulling off paint.

Paint trim in an orderly sequence, starting at the highest point. For an entire room, start with the crown molding and finish with the baseboard. When painting a door or window, start with the uppermost surfaces and work down. If you need to paint an entire window—including the sash and muntins—start with the inner surfaces, then move to the jambs and the casings as shown in the illustration on the previous page.

**PAINTING A DOOR CASING**

Paint head casing first, then paint sides

## FINISH-GRADE WORK

Finish-grade work is given either a clear top coat or stained and then sealed with clear finish. If possible, stain all wood before installation and allow it to dry thoroughly before handling it. Staining wood often raises the grain, so lightly sand stained pieces with 220-grit sandpaper before applying coats of clear finish.

There are three types of clear finishes.

**OIL:** These finishes are simply rubbed onto the workpieces. They enhance grain and color but they do not offer much protection against wear. An oil finish has a low sheen. You can oil workpieces before they are installed, then go back over the installations to set nails. Don't fill the holes with putty or filler; instead, use wax sticks that match the wood. Wipe up excess wax. Some oil finishes come premixed with stains or dyes to color the wood as the finish is applied.

**LACQUER:** Easy to apply, it comes in low-sheen, semigloss, and high-gloss. It is a fast-drying finish that can be handled in less than an hour after application. However, it is a volatile finish that releases lots of fumes—always work in a well-ventilated area and wear a respirator.

One of the advantages of lacquer is that the final appearance can be worked—putting on additional coats to give the finish a deeper, more lustrous sheen. To deepen the finish, let the lacquer dry thoroughly, then sand it lightly with 320-grit sandpaper. Remove dust with a tack rag, then recoat the workpiece. For best results, apply three or four coats, sanding lightly between coats. Polish the final coat with grade 0000 steel wool.

**POLYURETHANE:** One of the most popular finishes, it goes on easily and a single coating usually is enough. It is available in low-sheen, semigloss, and high-gloss. High-gloss polyurethanes, however, generally are considered too shiny for trim work. Of all the clear finishes, polyurethanes provide the best protection against moisture.

Polyurethanes can be difficult to apply. Their drying time varies widely with the amount of humidity in the air. Always let polyurethane finishes dry thoroughly before handling the parts.

# INDEX

96 **INDEX** *- eco cardogram*

Palm sanders, 28, 29
Paneling, wall, 46-47
  wainscoting, 48-51
Panel nails, 12
Picture frame casings, 60, 64
Picture rail, 9, 72-73
Pilot holes, drilling, 35
Pine, 6
Pipe clamps, 36
Planes, 30, 31
Plastic laminate flooring, 52, 54-55
Plinth blocks, 66, 67, 71
Plunge routers, 24-25
Plywood, 12
Polymer moldings, 8
Polyurethane finishes, 94
Polyvinyl acetate glues, 14
Poplar, 7
Preacher (jig), 70
Push sticks, use of, 23, 43
Putty, holes filled with, 92
Rabbets, 38, 39
Railings, stair, 56
Random-orbit (palm) sanders, 28, 29
Rasps, 30-31
Resorcinol glue, 14
Returns, miter-cut, 57, 64
Routers, 24-25
  flutes made on, 83, 84, 85

**S**
Saber saws, 22, 23
Safety, 17, 23, 42-43
Sanders, 28-29
Sanding before finishing, 92-93

Sandpaper, 15
Saws, hand, 16-17, 20-21
Saws, power, 22-23
  blade marks, removing, 82
  miters adjusted on, 41
  miters cut on, 69, 71, 74, 76
  safe use of, 23, 43
Scarf joints, 40
Screwdrivers, 13, 35
Screws, 12, 13
  holes for, 12, 13, 34, 35
  moldings installed with, 73
Sharpening
  chisels, 26, 27
  saws, 21
Sheet goods, 12
Sheet paneling, 46-47
Shelves, 86-89
  closet, 90-91
Softwoods vs. hardwoods, 6
Speed clamps, 36-37
Spring clamps, 36
Sprung molding, 74, 75
Squares (tools), 18-19
Stairs, 56-57
Stools, window, installing, 62, 63
Studs, locating, 73
Subfloors, 52

**T**
Table saws, 23
  blade marks, removing, 82
  miters cut on, 71, 74
  safe use of, 23, 43
Tear-out, 23, 31

Tongue-and-groove
  flooring, 52, 53, 54-55
  joints, 39
  paneling, 47, 48
Tools
  safety tips for, 23, 43
  *See also individual tools*
Trim and moldings. *See* Millwork
Try squares, 18, 19

**U**
Urea-formaldehyde glue, 14

**V**
Vinyl-wrapped molding, 8
Vises, 37

**W**
Wainscoting, 48-51
Wall-hung shelves, 88-89
Wall paneling, 46-47
  wainscoting, 48-51
Warped flooring boards, 55
Wet/dry sandpaper, 15
White oak, 7
Windows
  painting, 93
  trim, 60-65
  wainscoting and, 49, 51
Wood, kinds of, 6-7
Wood filler, use of, 92

## METRIC CONVERSIONS

| U.S. Units to Metric Equivalents | | | Metric Units to U.S. Equivalents | | |
|---|---|---|---|---|---|
| To Convert From | Multiply By | To Get | To Convert From | Multiply By | To Get |
| Inches | 25.4 | Millimeters | Millimeters | 0.0394 | Inches |
| Inches | 2.54 | Centimeters | Centimeters | 0.3937 | Inches |
| Feet | 30.48 | Centimeters | Centimeters | 0.0328 | Feet |
| Feet | 0.3048 | Meters | Meters | 3.2808 | Feet |
| Yards | 0.9144 | Meters | Meters | 1.0936 | Yards |
| Square inches | 6.4516 | Square centimeters | Square centimeters | 0.1550 | Square inches |
| Square feet | 0.0929 | Square meters | Square meters | 10.764 | Square feet |
| Square yards | 0.8361 | Square meters | Square meters | 1.1960 | Square yards |
| Acres | 0.4047 | Hectares | Hectares | 2.4711 | Acres |
| Cubic inches | 16.387 | Cubic centimeters | Cubic centimeters | 0.0610 | Cubic inches |
| Cubic feet | 0.0283 | Cubic meters | Cubic meters | 35.315 | Cubic feet |
| Cubic feet | 28.316 | Liters | Liters | 0.0353 | Cubic feet |
| Cubic yards | 0.7646 | Cubic meters | Cubic meters | 1.308 | Cubic yards |
| Cubic yards | 764.55 | Liters | Liters | 0.0013 | Cubic yards |

To convert from degrees Fahrenheit (F) to degrees Celsius (C), first subtract 32, then multiply by 5/9.

To convert from degrees Celsius to degrees Fahrenheit, multiply by 9/5, then add 32.